Walter Lynwood Fleming Lectures in Southern History

LOUISIANA STATE UNIVERSITY

STANLEY L. ENGERMAN

SLAVERY
EMANCIPATION
& FREEDOM

COMPARATIVE PERSPECTIVES

LOUISIANA STATE UNIVERSITY PRESS

BATON ROUGE

Published by Louisiana State University Press
Copyright © 2007 by Louisiana State University Press
All rights reserved
Manufactured in the United States of America
First printing

Designer: Michelle A. Garrod
Typeface: Adobe Caslon Pro
Printer and binder: Edwards Brothers, Inc.

Library of Congress Cataloging-in-Publication Data
Engerman, Stanley L.
  Slavery, emancipation, and freedom : comparative perspectives / Stanley L.
Engerman.
    p. cm. — (Walter Lynwood Fleming lectures in Southern history)
  Includes bibliographical references.
  ISBN-13: 978-0-8071-3236-4 (cloth : alk. paper) 1. Slavery. 2. Slavery—History.
3. Emancipation. I. Title.
  HT891.E55 2007
  306.3'6209—dc22

                                         2006100078

The paper in this book meets the guidelines for permanence and durability of
the Committee on Production Guidelines for Book Longevity of the Council
on Library Resources. ∞

For Judy

CONTENTS

This is a somewhat revised version of the Walter L. Fleming Lectures given at Louisiana State University, April 13–14, 2005. It was a great honor to be selected to give these lectures, and the visit to Baton Rouge was a most enjoyable and intellectually stimulating time. I wish to thank my hosts in the History Department, particularly Paul Paskoff, for their kindness and consideration.

Various drafts have been read and commented upon by several friends—David Brion Davis, Seymour Drescher, David Eltis, and Robert Steinfeld, and I am deeply grateful to each of them for the great help they provided. There were also useful critiques provided by two anonymous readers for the LSU Press. In addition I owe a substantial debt to a number of friends and colleagues who have long provided me with the information and insights on the set of problems discussed: Paul Cartledge, Kenneth Dean, Robert Fogel, the late Robert Gallman, Eugene Genovese, Max Hartwell, Barry Higman, Herbert Klein, Patrick O'Brien, Linda Levy Peck, the late Sherwin Rosen, and Kenneth Sokoloff.

Early drafts were typed, at the University of Rochester, Department of Economics by Kyla Barron, Lynn Enright, and Ronda Hirtzel, and by Ken Maher. Final revisions were made while visiting the W. E. B. Du Bois Institute for African and African American Research and the National Bureau of Economic Research. I should like to thank Rand Dotson and Lee C.

Sioles for help in the publication process and Marie Blanchard for her careful copyediting.

The historical examination of slavery poses numerous difficult problems in analysis. While there is no disagreement that the loss of freedom and control is a great evil, and the ending of slavery meant human progress, however limited it may have been, recent writings on slavery have pointed in new directions. The presentation of slaves as victims had emphasized the destructive nature of slavery and argued for limited cultural and psychological accomplishments by the enslaved. The more current discussions of slaves as active agents have focused on the accomplishments of slaves in various dimensions, and at one limit, seemingly minimized the impact of enslavement and the role of slave owners. Both views are consistent with the argument of slavery as an evil, although they can point in rather different directions. In trying to understand what slavery meant, and also what were the circumstances in which emancipation was achieved and how the ex-slave coped with freedom, there are two critical questions. First is the question posed in 1959 by Stanley Elkins, of determining what if any impact slavery had on the enslaved, and whether it was an impact that was very long-standing or one that could be quickly reversed by the provision of freedom. Second is the related question of whether descriptions of master behavior and of slave behavior are consistent psychologically. Neither question removes the point, however, that slavery was to be regarded as an evil to be abolished.

SLAVERY, EMANCIPATION, AND FREEDOM

One

SLAVERY IN WORLD PERSPECTIVE

THIS IS THE SIXTY-SEVENTH in the series of Fleming Lectures. They were established in 1936 in honor of an LSU history professor, most noted for his pro-southern work on Reconstruction. His publications include a still very important two-volume collection of documents on the history of Reconstruction in its "political, military, social, religious, educational and industrial" aspects. These were first published in 1906 and 1907.[1] Fleming's studies dealt with Reconstruction's effects on both whites and blacks, and he spent considerable time examining the links between the antebellum and postbellum eras (or as some call it, a replacement of one form of slavery by another). This link still seems not to have been given the attention it deserves for the understanding of slavery. Appropriately, most of the Fleming Lectures have dealt with southern history—generally with slavery, Reconstruction, and its aftermath.[2]

I

Slavery, according to the *Oxford English Dictionary*, was first referred to as the South's "peculiar institution" in 1852, and of course this term has become widely applied in subsequent years, being, for example, the title of the major 1956 history of southern slavery by Kenneth Stampp. According to the *Oxford English Dictionary* "peculiar" has overlapping but somewhat differ-

1. See Fleming (1906–1907).

2. For "a historiographic essay" on the first fifty-two of these lectures, see Noggle (1992).

ing meanings: "independent; particularly individual; strange; odd; distinctive." A *Times Literary Supplement* essay by Moses Finley in 1976 argued that, historically, free labor not slavery was the peculiar institution. The different definitions of "peculiar" featured in a response by Carl Degler, who claimed that the relevant meaning of "peculiar" for the antebellum South was "distinct and different" (having characteristics differentiating it from the North) but not necessarily strange or odd.[3] Whatever the outcome of this (generally ignored) linguistic debate, it seems to me that Finley's claim is very useful to historians, since it is meant to suggest the U.S. South, and antebellum slavery there, were not strange and odd, or deviant by standards of those times, as it certainly is by our twentieth- and twenty-first-century standards. "Slavery" has now become a term with no favorable connotations; it is used to indicate a wide range of always distasteful and abhorrent behaviors and is frequently applied to major abuses of human and labor rights today, whether permitted by law or not.

I want to begin by looking at the "peculiar institution" of the U.S. South from a context somewhat akin to Finley's—one stemming from the question of how unusual by historical and contemporary standards was slavery in the American South. This also relates to long-standing debates about the exceptionalism of American society, whether that exceptionalism is meant to present the United States as unusually good or unusually bad by world standards. This comparison is done not in an attempt to evaluate relative degrees of evil in different societies but rather to use the history of slavery to try to understand what most people of the times—slave owners, slaves, and non-slaveholding whites and blacks, South and North—understood about the

3. See Finley (1976).

presence of slavery and how they dealt with it, politically, culturally, and economically.

Slavery has existed in just about all parts of the world over just about all times.[4] Most societies have either been enslaved or enslavers at some time in the past, sometimes both at the same time. In the Americas, slavery existed among Native Americans and European settlers through the nineteenth century; in Europe, it was early on allowed for whites and it was acceptable to enslave other Europeans until about 1400; in both Asia and Africa, it was practiced before, during, and after the years of European colonial domination. In parts of the world such as Australia and the Pacific Islands, where slavery did not exist—at least slavery imposed by Europeans—it was because of the late date of settlement relative to the success of the Western antislavery movements as well as the availability of other forms of labor that could be coerced, such as indentured labor, convicts, or aborigines, to obtain the workers desired for settlement and production. Generally, as argued in 1900 by the Dutch ethnographer H. J. Nieboer, in most societies in which slavery did not exist this was not based on any moral grounds but pertained because labor productivity was so low that there was no surplus to be gained by enslaving others.[5] For Nieboer, societies with slavery had to have had a higher level of income than mere sub-

4. For detailed descriptions of slavery in different societies, it is easiest to start with four recent encyclopedic works on the history of slavery: Drescher and Engerman (1998), Finkelman and Miller (1998), M. Klein (2002), and J. Rodriguez (1997, 1999). For far-reaching examinations of slavery, see Nieboer (1971) and Patterson (1982), and for a thorough bibliography on slavery, see Miller (1999). For a magisterial presentation of the history and nature of slavery, drawing together a life's work on this topic, see D. B. Davis (2006).

5. Nieboer (1971), 417–27. For a formalization of this argument, see Domar (1970).

sistence, and freedom at a subsistence level was not necessarily an economic or social gain to the formerly enslaved.

Slavery was clearly not peculiar—or unique—to the descendants of European settlers in the American South in the nineteenth century. It had existed in all areas of the Americas, both before and after European arrival, characterizing many of the Native American societies, with both large and small populations. The earlier existence of Native American enslavement of other Native Americans, generally war captives, made the transition to European settler enslavement of Native Americans easier, as the basis for the trade was already there.[6]

As late as 1820, there were still over ten thousand slaves in New York State (to be freed in 1827 as a result of legislation passed in 1817), and in 1830 some twelve of thirteen northern states still had some slaves listed in the federal census—ranging from one in Massachusetts to 2,254 in New Jersey. In 1860 there were still "18 colored apprentices for life in New Jersey," listed in the slave column of the census compendium.[7] And, lest some northerners see this limited number of slaves as providing some moral high ground, it was, by historical standards, relatively recently that slavery had been legal in all North American colonies, including those in the North. The reason for limited slavery in the North seemed based more on economic factors than on any moral reservations. And, when slavery in the North was to be ended, it was only by the most gradual of measures. Adam

6. For some discussion of Native American enslavement of other Native Americans in different parts of the Americas, see Donald (1997); Lauber (1913), 25–47; Clendinnen (1991), 30, 52, 78–79, 98–101, 163, which includes a discussion of Aztec human sacrifice; Brooks (2002), 45–51, 180–97, 350–52; Lockhart and Schwartz (1983), 41–42; and Gallay (2002), 8–10, 25–29.

7. Kennedy (1862), 127, 128; Walker (1872), 16. These were attributed to New Jersey's "act to abolish slavery, passed April 18, 1846." The 1830 figure for Massachusetts was possibly a typographical error.

Smith had cynically suggested regarding "the late resolution of the Quakers in Pennsylvania to set at liberty all their [N]egro slaves" that it "may satisfy us that their number cannot be very great."[8] To Smith the demand curve for morality was downward sloping, a hypothesis that also provides a reasonable explanation for the time pattern of later slave emancipations. Smith, it might be noted, was not optimistic that slavery would ever be abolished on political grounds, since those who would legislate on the legality of slave ownership were often the owners of slaves; nor did he anticipate a voluntary ending on economic grounds.

The first northern state to abolish slavery (in 1777), Vermont, had a constitutional provision allowing for a period as "servants, slaves, or apprentices" until age twenty-one for males or eighteen for females. The next two, New Hampshire and Massachusetts, did have immediate (subject to judicial decisions) uncompensated emancipation, but these three states freed very few slaves. In the five northern states (Pennsylvania, Rhode Island, Connecticut, New York, and New Jersey) that had emancipation legislation passed between 1780 and 1804, it applied only to those born after a certain date, thus freeing none of the existing slaves and leaving the numbers of slaves unchanged. Those born after that date were apprenticed to their mothers' owners for varying periods of time, from fifteen to thirty years, depending on the state, and sometimes varying with gender, a policy that was to make it financially worthwhile for owners to raise these children while imposing minimal costs on taxpayers. It also provided what many thought necessary, a period of training and education for the freed blacks.[9]

8. Smith (1976), 1:388. On Smith, see Drescher (2002).

9. On northern emancipation schemes, see Zilversmit (1967) and Fogel and Engerman (1974b). It is estimated that Vermont had a total of 19 blacks in 1771; New Hampshire 656 "slaves" in 1775; and Massachusetts (and Maine) 5,249

Further, before the Civil War, most northern states maintained, or had newly imposed, strict limits on free black voting and education. Prohibitions on the right to enter and settle existed in several states, sometimes persisting even after the start of the Civil War.[10] These schemes of northern emancipation, freeing none of those presently slaves but only, after some delay, the after-born, were to be a most frequent means of emancipation throughout the Americas, and also elsewhere. It was applied in most South and Central American nations, including Cuba (in 1870, made retroactive to 1868) and in Brazil (1871), where it was called the "law of the free womb." The important debate on immediate versus gradual emancipation, based on the presumed effects of enslavement, was to be a long-standing and contentious one, and one which, some argued, pointed to the advantage of a gradual process, both in terms of numbers freed and the length of time until an individual's freedom was achieved.

Within the Americas, slavery remained an ongoing and expanding institution well past 1860, with the final ending of legal slavery in the Dutch colonies coming in 1863 (and ex-slave apprenticeship ending in 1873), in Puerto Rico in 1873 (with apprenticeship ending in 1876), in Cuba in 1886 (where the Moret Law,

---

"blacks and mulattos" in 1776. In 1780, these states accounted for about 1.0 percent of U.S. blacks, and blacks were about 1.3 percent of their total population. Carter et al. (2006), 5:651–53, 657–59. For a discussion of these and other emancipations, see Engerman (1995).

10. See, for example, Litwack (1961). For 1813 Illinois legislation regarding black exclusion, see Philbrick (1950), 91–92, where the punishment for a black refusal to leave within fifteen days was to be whipped, "not exceeding thirty-nine stripes, nor less than twenty-five stripes." Whipping was still an important form of punishment in the U.S. Navy as well as for child labor in England. On the persistence of whipping in nonslave societies, see Fogel and Engerman (1974a), 2:155–58. For the constraints on relocating ex-slaves in the North during the Civil War, see Voegeli (2003).

a variant of the "free womb" law, was passed in 1870 and applied to births after 1868), and in Brazil in 1888 (after the "law of the free womb" was introduced in 1871).[11] Cuba and Brazil had received large numbers in the transatlantic slave trade long after the United States and Britain ended their slave trades in 1808, with the trade to Brazil ending in 1851 and that to Cuba in 1867. The ending of the slave trade was due more to British political pressure than to any economic decline in the area. The numbers of slaves arriving in the Americas in the 1830s and 1840s were close to the numbers that arrived before 1808.[12] Even where slavery itself had ended in the Caribbean colonies before the American Civil War, it was generally only recent—the 1830s for the British colonies and the late 1840s for the Swedish, Danish, and French. The one exceptional case, St. Domingue, later Haiti, had constitutionally ended slavery in 1804, after its successful slave uprising. This ending was two years after the French, having previously ended slavery in their other Caribbean colonies in 1794, had reintroduced slavery there in 1802. Several of the newly independent Spanish areas of South and Central America also provided compensation, via cash payments and apprenticeships, when ending slavery after the 1820s, although the process of emancipation was not completed in the last emancipating nation until the 1860s.[13] These emancipations throughout the Americas (and, it should be noted, the roughly simultaneous

11. See Engerman (1995). See also Ziskind (1993). Among the schemes discussed by the Dutch, but not utilized, was a proposal to have the ex-slaves pay cash to their former owners to pay for their freedom with the earnings from work on plantations owned by the state. See Kuitenbrouwer (1995).

12. On the magnitude of the transatlantic slave trade, see Eltis (2001). The Danish decree of 1792 ending the slave trade allowed ten years before the slave trade was ended. See Green-Pedersen (1975).

13. On Latin American emancipations and their provisions, see H. Klein (1986), Rout (1976), and Engerman (1995).

ending of serfdom in Europe), generally occurred with compensation to the owners with the exceptions of, initially, Haiti, several Latin American countries, and the United States.[14] Haiti later did pay compensation to France. Compensation for emancipation could take the form of cash, bonds, or labor time paid to the slave owners, who were also allowed to keep their land. The freed slaves and serfs everywhere generally received no economic benefits but the crucial one of freedom.

Cuba, in the 1850s, had become a booming, flexible economy, shifting crops and plantation locations to become the world's leading sugar cane producer, and, despite the continued import of slaves from Africa, slave prices reached all-time peaks.[15] So great was the demand for labor, and so limited relative to Cuban needs was the supply of slaves obtained from Africa (due, in part, to the British blockade of the African coast, however limited in effectiveness) that, between 1847 and 1874, the Cubans also imported about 125,000 indentured laborers (almost all male) from China. The end of this flow was owing to Chinese actions ending out-migration, rather than to any limits on arrivals imposed by Cubans.[16] Similarly, the Indian Ocean island of Mauritius, almost immediately after slave emancipation, began to import indentured labor from India to permit the continuation of sugar production.[17]

The years after the 1840s also saw a rapid expansion and adjustment in the Brazilian economy, with rising prices of slaves,

14. On the beliefs and behavior under European serfdom, see Blum (1978).

15. See Bergad et al. (1995), Bergad (2004), Moreno Fraginals (1976), Moreno Fraginals et al. (1983), Scott (1985), and H. Klein (1986).

16. See Helly intro. (1993), Corbitt (1971), and Moreno Fraginals (1976). On the British blockade against the slave trade, see Eltis (1987)

17. Allen (1999), 15–17, 55–75.

until the onset of the legislation leading to emancipation.[18] Until 1851, Brazil was receiving slaves in the transatlantic trade. The ending of the trade was due to British political and naval pressures, as was also to be the case, about sixteen years later, in Cuba. In neither case was the ending of the international slave trade due to a decline in the demand for export products or for slaves. Brazil was, after the 1820s, readjusting its economy from the dominance of slavery and sugar in the northeast to become the world's largest coffee exporter, with production on the basis of slave labor taking place in Brazil's southeast. Ending slavery required legislation, with the "law of the free womb" in 1871 and several interim measures, until final emancipation in 1888.[19]

Based on economic developments in Cuba and Brazil, not to mention the U.S. South—the world's largest producer of cotton at the middle of the nineteenth century—one can understand why slave owners and many others at the time, unlike many today, found it hard to believe that economically slavery was ineffectual and wealth-destroying. Such economic expansion contrasted with areas in which slavery had ended, such as Haiti—once the richest part of the world but now on its way to becoming the lowest income area of the Americas, with considerable and prolonged political instability. Similarly, the British West Indies, in the 1850s, were still stagnating, for the most part. The British Islands were unable to compete in sugar exports with Brazil and Cuba without preferential tariff protection, which was, however, maintained only for a limited period.[20] In the 1860s some British colonies in Africa, Asia, and Ocea-

18. Bergad (1999), and for an analysis of the effect of anticipated emancipation on slave prices, see De Mello (1992). See also Mattoso et al. (1986).

19. Conrad (1972), Eltis (1987), and H. Klein (1986).

20. See Green (1976), for a discussion of these issues.

nia started to expand sugar production with the use of indentured labor, brought in mainly from China and India, but also from the Portuguese islands, Africa, and elsewhere. This followed the earlier, 1830s attraction of indentured labor from India to the island of Mauritius, which led to a rapid growth there in sugar production. The one British post-emancipation success proclaimed by the antislavery people, Barbados, expanded economically because of high population density and low wages and was soon to start experiencing out-migration to elsewhere in the Caribbean, and later to the U.S. North.[21]

In regard to the United States, many of the arguments made, then and now, for the weakness of the slave economy were more in the form of long-term forecasts to argue for antebellum economic backwardness and decline. These claims often reflected contentions that presumed a rather long time span before the predicted events occurred, and did not suggest any immediate major financial worries. Some pointed to the limits to the economic growth of slavery that would result from a limit on geographic expansion, but this was often presented without a belief that decline was to be soon anticipated. The costs of relative shortfall in southern urbanization and industrialization, even if correct at the time, did not mean that the system was about to collapse. Perhaps the most famous of these economic claims, by the Irish economist John Elliot Cairnes, was based on projections of land-labor ratios. The end of slavery, he argued, was not

21. See Beckles (1990), and for the changing pattern of emigration, see Roberts (1955). Barbados had low slave prices prior to emancipation and low wages afterwards. In the emancipation debates, Barbados argued for compensation based on the number, not the prices, of slaves. See Engerman (1984, 1996). For a positive assessment of the Barbados achievement by antislavery advocates, see Sewell (1862) and Sturge and Harvey (1968). By 1900, Barbados was experiencing emigration to the urban north of the United States.

imminent on economic grounds but was dependent on political events. He argued that while, no doubt, the trend was clear, actual emancipation would occur only "by a gradual but sure process" and "in due time," with "ultimate extinction" being "at least a quarter of a century" in the future, at least on the basis of economic considerations. In that time period, however, Cairnes feared a strengthening of the South's political and economic power, which might cause further delays.[22] In 1858, Lincoln posited the "ultimate extinction" of slavery in not "less than a hundred years at the least," but only if there was not allowed any movement of slavery into the territories, and he believed this timing and method was the best way for emancipation to occur, for both slave owners and slaves. Slavery was, he commented in the 1850s, not then declining but was then "in its state of progress as it is now driving, as it has been driven for the last five years." Lincoln argued that the founding fathers had believed that slavery was placed on the road to an early extinction by the Constitution, but this had not occurred owing to "the invention of the cotton-gin." He omitted, however, to mention any possibility of some similar unanticipated technical change in the post-1858 period, changes that might still further postpone slavery's demise.[23]

Thus, looking within the South and elsewhere in the Americas, southern slave owners did not need to believe that theirs was a peculiar institution even in contrast with the North, or

22. Cairnes (1969), 274, 276–77, 350.

23. Lincoln (1989a), 603–4, 677. The basic Malthusian argument of Cairnes and of Lincoln based on population density was also then widely used to forecast the decline of free labor societies in the North and elsewhere and was made central to American history by Frederick Jackson Turner. The argument was not unique to describing the antebellum South; it was very widely held and was applied to the North and Europe as well.

that it was unable to survive economically in the contemporary world. Those slave owners with any interest in the biblical, classical, and medieval worlds also knew that the existence of slavery had a much longer and geographically extensive history than just the nineteenth-century American South.[24] Slavery was obviously not unique to the American South, but it was clearly among the most ubiquitous and long-standing of all human institutions influencing population and labor supply. It went back to biblical times and, with variations, it is argued by some still to exist today in the form of "wage slavery," "debt slavery," "child slavery," "spousal slavery," "sex slavery," as well as numerous other "slaveries." Whether they argue that the term "slavery" is used mainly for rhetorical purposes aimed at advocating the suppression of something evil (due to labor controls, population controls, or income levels), or whether it is meant to suggest that, legally and otherwise, today's slavery is like slavery in the past, it is clear that some still consider slavery of some form to be rather widespread today in many parts of the world.

II

The fall of the Confederacy did not, of course, mark the ending of slavery in the Americas and elsewhere. As we have seen, slavery in the Dutch colonies in the Americas persisted until 1863, with apprenticeship until 1873; slavery in Puerto Rico did not end until 1873, while apprenticeship lasted until 1876; Cuba and Brazil ended slavery in 1886 and 1888, respectively, after frequent legislation concerning the "free womb," apprenticeship, and emancipation. But even these endings did not mean the

24. See, for example, the detailed discussion of the references made by the southern intellectual elite to ancient and medieval slavery in Fox-Genovese and Genovese (2005), 249–328, as well as the discussion in Genovese (1989).

worldwide end of slavery, and in parts of Asia and Africa slavery legally persisted into the twentieth century. For example, slavery in Thailand ended in 1905 and in China only in 1910. Slavery did not end in the Turkish Republic until 1924. Slavery did not end in the Arabian Peninsula until 1970. In North Africa, Mauritania has effectively outlawed slavery at least three times in the twentieth century—in 1905 (by the French), 1960, and 1980, and yet some form of slavery still apparently continues to exist there, as it seems to some to also persist today in Sudan and Niger.[25] The numbers of slaves in the world at the start of the twentieth century was not small in number or in social impact. It has been estimated that, in 1850, there were more slaves in Africa than in the Americas, and in 1900 there were more legally defined slaves in Africa than had existed at any single year in the Americas, with smaller but still significant numbers in Asia.[26] In the twentieth century, Nazi Germany and the Soviet Union have been described as having European forms of modern slavery, raising greatly the estimated number of slaves. Works such as that by Kevin Bales have drawn considerable attention with

25. For dates, see M. Klein (1993, 2002), Rodriguez (1997, 1999), Miers and Roberts (1988), Watson (1980), and Miers (2003). Miers discusses Mauritania on pages 418–20. The present-day pattern of slavery in Niger is described in the *Economist*, March 12, 2005, 49. Until quite recently slavery was apparently illegal, but there was no legal penalty for slave ownership. See Miers (2003), Bales (1999).

26. M. Klein (1998), 252–57, estimates a French West African slave population in the first decade of the twentieth century of between 3 and 3.5 million. Lovejoy and Hogendorn (1993), 1, estimate that the slave population of the Sokoto Caliphate (northern Nigeria) at that time was "in excess of 1 million and perhaps more than 2.5 million people." Manning (1990), 23, estimates that "the slave population in Africa was roughly equal in size to the New World slave population from the seventeenth to the early nineteenth centuries," and "after about 1850, there were more slaves in Africa than in the New World." The population of Africa was probably below that of the Americas in 1900.

estimates of what is called modern slavery in the range of 20–30 million.[27]

Not only did slavery long exist, a large-scale movement of slaves and other forms of coerced labor from one region to others, often distant, was a long-standing historical phenomenon that started early and continued late. The transatlantic slave trade of some 10–12 million Africans was carried on by Europeans, from the middle of the fifteenth century until the mid-nineteenth century. While the "Middle Passage" and the productive use of slave labor in the Americas were activities undertaken in response to demands by Europeans, because of disease and military factors within Africa the original capture of slaves and the march to the coast was undertaken by African capturers and traders, who benefited from rising prices paid by Europeans for slaves and from the improved terms-of-trade for African merchants.[28] There were perhaps roughly equal numbers, as in the transatlantic trade, moved in the trade from southern and central Africa to northern Africa and the Middle East, via the Sahara and the Red Sea, although over a longer period of years.[29] Of still uncertain magnitude, but possibly larger than the two trades mentioned, was the internal slave trade in Africa, in large measure sending slaves away from their areas of residence to relocate to live and work elsewhere. While the numbers in this trade are very uncertain, several scholars have estimated that, of the African captives in the eighteenth and nineteenth centuries, somewhere between one-third and one-half of captives went

27. See Drescher (1996); Bales (1999), 8–10, 23; and the essays in van den Anker (2004). The problem of definition is complex, since many of those considered slaves by Bales (15) are "enslaved for only a few months."

28. See Eltis (1987) and Rodney (1972).

29. See Lovejoy (1983) as well as Austen (1979).

into the internal slave trade and were not sent out of Africa.[30] Other long-distance movements, such as that of slaves from western to eastern Europe in medieval times and from the Mediterranean region to ancient Greece and Rome, preceded the movements from and within Africa, and similarly long-distance movements characterized other slave societies as well as those societies utilizing indentured labor.

Thus it is clear that slavery as a legal institution was not peculiar to the Americas or to the American South and that both the African knowledge of enslaving and the African experience of having been enslaved did not require the arrival of Europeans or Americans, even if patterns of African and American, and also Native American, slavery had some quite important social and cultural differences. Indeed the existence of slavery in Africa and among Native Americans probably permitted the rapid response to emerging European demands, as well as providing a cultural background for living as slaves to others. These points underlie Finley's description of slavery as a rather omnipresent institution, historically found in most societies, at most times.

A look at the many historical cases described by H. J. Nieboer and by Orlando Patterson suggests the ubiquity of slave societies. Historically, in most societies the primary source of labor used in production was not slaves or serfs but nominally

30. For estimates see Manning (1990), 47, who uses a demographic model to infer that retained slaves were "over half of the total number of slaves exported." See also Manning (1988), 26. Lovejoy (1983), 64, applies Manning's model to estimate that exported slaves accounted for about 45 percent of the total enslaved population. While these estimates are based on uncertain assumptions, they are suggestive of possible orders of magnitude. The early existence of the internal slave trade and the trade to North Africa permitted a relatively rapid development of the transatlantic slave trade, resting as it did on existing networks and not requiring a new set of organizational innovations.

free labor (although often with some form of legal or nonlegal coercion). The presence of slavery has been but one extreme form of persistent labor coercion, including also serfdom in areas where— for some reason, economic or otherwise, no doubt reflecting demographic and settlement issues—slavery did not develop.[31] At times, free labor meant working for oneself; at times it meant working for wages or other compensation from an employer. The role of economic and political coercion has, of course, characterized most societies in the past. In the late eighteenth century, the astute British observer Arthur Young claimed that over 90 percent of the world's population could be regarded as unfree or coerced (to Young, "miserable slaves of despotic tyrants"). Adam Smith suggested similar orders of magnitude with a similar geographic breakdown, since slavery had been abolished only in a "small part of Europe." Those considered unfree by Young and by Smith lived mainly outside of western Europe and mainland North America.[32]

Clearly, by the standards of the Americas and, indeed, even by world standards, slavery in the American South was not an unusual institution. In 1860, about 12.6 percent of the U.S. population was enslaved (and about 14 percent was black), and, even in the slave states, the ratio was about 35 percent. This was simi-

31. Serfdom generally meant legally binding to the land a population already present, while slavery frequently meant the movement of labor from one location to another. Serfs presumably could not be sold apart from the land they worked on, but slaves could. Given the importance of geographic movement in the attack on slavery, the argument against serfdom was to this extent weakened. In addition, serfs and their masters were generally from a similar ethnic group, and serfs, even with their limited political and social power, were not outsiders in the same way that slaves were. On serfdom, see Blum (1978).

32. See Young (1772), 19–22, and Smith (1978), 1:181. Smith further argues, in a critique of "republican government," that "it is indeed almost impossible that it

lar to the other large slave power in the Americas, Brazil, at about 33 percent, as well as to the earlier major slave societies of Greece and Rome.[33] As important as slavery may have been economically, these areas all had larger nonslave populations, serving as both a source of protection against slave revolt and as a major source of the production of goods and services, though not generally of plantation export output. The truly unusual cases of slavery were in the Caribbean, particularly in those areas settled by the British, French, Danish, Swedish, and Dutch, where the populations by the end of the eighteenth century were generally about 90 percent black slave and only 10 percent free whites, a situation posing major issues for control that, except for one case (Haiti), was apparently solved by slave-owning whites.[34] These areas were either islands or (like Belize and the Guianas) coastal colonies with favorable conditions for sugar production and exporting. Nevertheless, the French and British settlements were not initially based on sugar production and slave labor, the first settlements being generally by white labor producing tobacco. The transition to the effective use of slave labor could take as long as a half century.

The Caribbean presented a high slave-to-free ratio, one that no other society, at least none at that time, had ever achieved.

[slavery] should ever be totally or generally abolished," particularly in a republican government, since this "would be to deprive the far greater part of the subjects, and the nobles in particular, of the chief and most valuable parts of their substance" (187). When slavery had been previously abolished, "it was owing to some peculiar circumstances" (186), although these are not detailed. On Young, Smith, and other contemporary sources, see Drescher (1987), 16–18.

33. Carter et al. (2006), 1:48, and Finley (1998), 147–48, for these breakdowns.

34. For population estimates, see Engerman and Higman (1998) and Engerman (2000).

The one set of exceptions to this 90 percent slave population in the Caribbean were the Spanish-speaking areas (Cuba, Puerto Rico, Santo Domingo), where the late development of sugar production, influenced by the earlier restrictive Spanish policies, meant lower black-white ratios. Nevertheless, Cuba was nearly 50 percent slave by the middle of the nineteenth century, owing to its delayed but by then highly successful sugar boom.

III

I have gotten this far without any attempt to define what slavery is, presuming that all know the key points of the legal concept. As always, definitions are complex, and those for slavery usually have both legal and economic components, including some combination of poor living conditions, coercion in laboring, and loss of various social and political rights, all of which restrict the choices possible to individuals. To some, slavery is one—extreme—end of a spectrum; to others, slavery represents a distinct system not comparable to anything else. Thus to describe slavery as a unique institution will upset those who see controls and coercion in other labor systems, while to point to similarities with other coercive systems can be seen as somehow limiting the evils of slavery. And, to others, even slavery itself presents a spectrum of behavior and treatment. Some constraints are due to nature and some are imposed by other members of the population. Perhaps no single definition covers all legal aspects, and different aspects require differences in emphasis to be useful. Nevertheless, the most crucial and frequently utilized aspect of enslavement, and the most widely accepted, is the right to buy and sell individuals, its permanent or at least lifelong condition, and the inheritability of the status. Important are questions of the legal terms and the extent of enforcement. The lifetime and inherited conditions mean we can put aside, on the one hand, convicts and indentured servants with time limitations and also the cases both of those athletes who can be bought and sold and of those actors and directors who, under the old Hollywood studio system, could be rented out. Such groups have frequently used the analogy with slavery in pursuit of contractual rights.[35]

The control over slaves meant the owners had the ability to determine location of life and work, as well as the type of labor performed. Various constraints regarding what masters could do to slaves have always existed in actuality, but these were often, legally, at the sufferance of the masters and reflected both the particular aims that the masters sought to achieve and what free society regarded as acceptable behavior and might be enforced by social pressure. To say that the place and type of labor is controlled is not to claim that owners need not worry about

35. See Lowenfish (1991) on the history of the reserve clause in baseball and the use of the term "baseball slave" in the 1880s. For a rough estimate of trends in exploitation in baseball from 1876 to 1973: with the reserve clause in effect, the ratio of baseball salaries to manufacturing wages was in the range of 3–5 to 1; currently with free agency it is about 50 to 1. (It is estimated that the average rate of player exploitation was about 85 percent under the reserve clause and fell to less than one-quarter with free agency.) Ava Gardner, the actress, in the era of the studio system regarded herself as a "wage slave" because, while she received a salary of $60,000 for three months, she was rented out to make *The Barefoot Contessa* for $200,000; plus her studio gained a share of the movie's profits. See Gardner (1990), 195. Judge Frank, in the Danny Gardella case in the 1940s concerning the enforcement of the reserve clause in baseball, claimed that the contract "possesses characteristics shockingly repugnant to moral principles that, at least since the War Between the States, have been basic in America, as shown by the Thirteenth Amendment to the Constitution, condemning 'involuntary servitude.'" Quirk and Fort (1992), 188. He also pointed out that "if the players be regarded as quasi-peons, it is of no moment that they are well paid; only the totalitarian-minded will believe that high pay excuses virtual slavery." The Hollywood studio system was ended by a case brought by the actress Olivia de Haviland in the 1940s under the California Debt Peonage Law.

specific work incentives to influence effort and output in the place of work. There are aspects to this incentive problem in which the issue for slaves is quite similar to that of free workers. These were worked out by some ancient Greeks, notably Xenophon, and most subsequent slave owners were concerned with working out appropriate arrangements to encourage output from slaves.[36] When Adam Smith commented that slave labor was inefficient because it lacked incentives, it became a very popular, widely used antislavery argument, but what it most clearly showed was that it was doubtful that Smith had ever seen or studied an operating plantation.[37]

Slavery has been quite frequently, but not always, reserved to individuals who are believed to be, or can credibly be argued to be, outsiders, not members of a given society.[38] To be regarded as an outsider does not necessarily mean that a per-

36. See Xenophon (1990), 289–359, "The Estate-Manager," particularly 297, 302, 307, 334, 336. See also Engerman (2002b), and for related discussions of labor force management of slaves in the U.S. South, see Breeden (1980). Xenophon claimed that "slaves need good prospects for the future just as much as free men—or even more—to make them prepared to stay put," and, while noting the similarity of training slaves and lower animals, he anticipated that "you'll get plenty of results by gratifying their bellies in accordance with their desires." Aristotle (1935), 32–34, claimed that "it is a good thing that all slaves should have before them the prospect of receiving their freedom as a reward." Cicero (1913), 45, states that "they give us no bad rule who bid us treat our slaves as we should our employees; they must be required to work; they must be given their dues." See also the various quotes in Garnsey (1996), 87–97, and Engerman (2002b) discussing treatment of slaves and incentives to labor. For an examination of the great appeal of Xenophon in the antebellum South, see Fox-Genovese and Genovese (2005), 366, 745–46.

37. See Smith (1976), 1:386–88. Smith's blanket statement on slave labor is not consistent with his argument on the superior management of slave labor by the French compared to the British (2:586–89).

38. See Finley (1998) and Patterson (1982) for statements of this argument.

son would become a slave, but rather that he or she could be treated differently from insiders, in being allowed to suffer punishments different from those meted out to members of the insider society. After all, outsiders cannot only be enslaved but can be excluded, discriminated against, segregated, geographically isolated, imprisoned, assimilated, allowed self-determination, or killed, among other forms of treatment. There are cases in which outsiders were enslaved to provide labor, but other times outsiders were excluded or forced to be geographically distant, which kept them out of the productive labor force, presumably in the interests of other ends, such as population homogeneity or raising labor incomes.[39] While it is correct that in most cases those enslaved are held to be outsiders, not all of those regarded as outsiders do become slaves, however difficult may be their treatment within society.

The outsider distinction has played a major role in antislavery debates. The basic economic, psychological, and moral arguments against slavery have a long history, with similar points to be found among Greeks and Romans as among nineteenth-century British and American antislavery advocates. Adam Smith was not the first writer to raise the issue of slave labor incentives, and discussion of the effects of enslavement on the slaves (and also on their owners and their families) has a similarly long history. Thus the nineteenth century presents no really new economic, psychological, or moral arguments for the end-

39. For a brief discussion of the implications of racism for slavery and other forms of behavior, see Engerman (forthcoming). On the role of the racist antislavery argument, wishing to exclude rather than enslave those of a different race, see, for the U.S., Locke (1901), starting with the very early argument for Delaware made by Usselinx (9–20), and for the role played in nineteenth-century Cuba, see Murray (1980), 128–29, 178–80, 204–6, with its argument for "pure blood" and racial homogeneity.

ing of slavery but rather was based on who could now be considered as insiders, and who could end the system.[40]

Moreover, the characteristic feature of the outsider has shifted over time, and the present familiar exclusive focus on race (or what some consider to be race) is a product of recent centuries and is prevalent mainly among Europeans and Americans.[41] Certainly the relevant categorization of outsider for African enslavement of Africans is not race as usually understood. Nathan Huggins [1977], for example, has argued that Africans had enslaved other Africans because, until the twentieth century, they did not believe that they belonged to the same tribe.[42] Others, earlier, were defined as outsiders according to nationality, religion, intelligence and capabilities, ethnicity, or tribal

40. The early argument was to treat slaves as "human," since slavery was regarded as a vile and contemptible institution, and masters should treat slaves "with some basic kindness and justice." It was claimed that "freedom was the dearest and most valuable of all benefits" (Burns, 4:983). The Siete Partidas further states that "servitude is the vilest and most contemptible thing that can exist among men, for the reason that man, who is the most noble and free among all the creatures that God made, is brought by means of it under the power of another, so that the latter can do with him what he pleases" (Burns, 4:901). It was "contrary to natural reason" (Burns, 4:977). Nevertheless, the master "should not kill or wound him . . . nor should he strike him in a way contrary to natural reason, or put him to death by starvation," except under certain extreme conditions (Burns, 4:979). An excellent source for many of these arguments is Garnsey (1996), particularly 53–64, on "Slave systems criticized." Homer had claimed that slaves are only one-half a freeman, an estimate of relative productivity and of personhood that persisted into the nineteenth century with many advocates.

41. See, in particular, Fields (1990) on the claim that race has been a category representing an ideology, not one representing any reality. See also Vaughan (1995), 136–74. On the role of color in Islam, see D. B. Davis (2006), 56–64.

42. On the enslavement of black Africans by other black Africans, see the comment of Huggins (1977), 20: "The racial irony was lost on African merchants, who saw themselves as selling people other than their own. The distinctions of

grouping.[43] And, as Richard Hellie describes for sixteenth-century Russian slavery, a rewritten history was needed to define the enslaved Russians with appropriate characteristics to be considered as outsiders.[44] While white Europeans may have avoided enslavement in the Americas and in Europe, there were possibly one million white slaves (mainly from Italy, Spain, and Portugal) in Algiers and elsewhere in North Africa from the sixteenth to the eighteenth centuries.[45]

While most slavery, particularly in the Americas, was clearly involuntary, in that the enslaved were generally wartime captives and did not elect to enter this status (unless we regard as meaningful the choice between living in enslavement or suffering death), the issue of slavery is complicated by the longtime existence in many places of what can be regarded, at least in terms

---

tribe were more real to them than race, a concept that was yet to be refined by nineteenth- and twentieth-century Western rationalists." Also of note is the trip to West Africa organized by the Dutch anthropologist Silvia W. de Groot, to take Surinam Maroon chiefs to their areas of origin in West Africa. Whatever rapport had been anticipated was weakened when the Maroons indicated their belief "that their forefathers had been carried off as slaves with the help of their brothers, and so there was some compensation due them." And, responding to a "delicious meal," it was commented that, "probably it's been paid for by the money made by selling us as slaves." De Groot (2003), 16, 27.

43. For a description of Islamic attitudes regarding race and slavery, see Lewis (1990), 5–6, 16–27, 36. Lewis argues that the Koran "assumes the existence of slavery" but also "urges . . . kindness to the slave and recommends . . . his liberation by purchase or manumission." Although there were initially many white slaves, over time the share of "blacks" enslaved from Africa increased.

44. See Hellie (1982), 57–64, 389–96.

45. See Wolf (1979), Allison (1995), and R. Davis (2003). Davis (2003), 3–27, estimates there were over one million white slaves captured between 1530 and 1750. Unlike most slaves sent from Africa, many white slaves were, in effect, ransomed by European governments and religious and private groups.

of legality, as voluntary slavery. Self-sale and sale of children (of course, a question remains whether or not a parent's sale of children should be regarded as voluntary, from the child's perspective) have been practiced in many societies, and voluntary slavery was widely debated in the seventeenth and eighteenth centuries.[46] The case for volunteering for slavery was based on the choice between enslavement as opposed to starvation or other causes of death. Voluntary slavery was not advocated, except in cases of necessity due to very low incomes or as a response to severe famine. In the absence of public or private welfare systems, or of acceptable sources of employment, as a means to redistribute incomes or to offset the subsistence problem, slavery was considered the one major alternative. In times of great political instability, slavery, and serfdom, might seem preferred alternatives to freedom in order to provide protection and survival.[47] The voluntary slaves were less often outsiders, and there were apparently some differences in treatment and more opportunities to obtain freedom than in the case of involuntary slavery.

The distinction between outsiders and insiders has played a significant role in the study of slavery, but that distinction is not

46. See Engerman (2007). This debate concerns the role of natural rights and the meaning of the choice between slavery and death.

47. Thus slavery has been described as "the Indian Poor Law" for its role in helping avoid starvation. Temperley (1972), 96. Refusal to accept freedom in twentieth-century Africa was attributed to "free" status resulting in lower standards of working and living, and failing to maintain some of the traditional privileges of slaves as well as the desire to avoid the imposed coercion of required state labor. G. Campbell (2003), xxiv–xxvii. See also Miers (2004). For a longer discussion of the incidence and importance of voluntary slavery in the modern world, see Engerman (2007). The subject was touched on by many early political theorists, such as Bodin, Hobbes, Grotius, Pufendorf, and Locke, with the general conclusion that it was acceptable in the absence of other means of providing subsistence for individuals and family members.

necessarily the only consideration that influences moral behavior and belief within a society. The insider-outsider distinction can lead to some unexpected moral stances and puzzling questions. By 1400, western Europeans had stopped the enslavement of other western Europeans and, within England, serfdom had also ended.[48] This did not mean, however, that slavery and labor coercion were ended, but only that, for Europeans, slavery, on the Continent and overseas, was reserved to those Africans and Asians who were regarded as outsiders. And in this interval, slavery still existed in Asia, Africa, and the Americas. Over the next four centuries, about 10 to 12 million Africans were taken to the New World as slaves, with little thought given in most of this period to introducing policies ending the transoceanic movement, or else of freeing the slaves in the Americas (by Europeans or by ransoming by Africans), or of returning the slaves to Africa. At this same time, however, these European nations were almost continuously at war with each other, and probably suffered about 13 million casualties in the wars between 1500 and 1900, in addition to the many more injured and the civilians who died because of wartime disruptions.[49] France alone suffered about 5 million military deaths in the years between

48. See Karras (1988), 122–63, and for a discussion of the ending of English serfdom, see Hilton (1969). Since, at times, serfdom in Europe was voluntarily entered into in exchange for defense and protection provided the serf, the development of larger political units and nation-states in Europe served to limit the importance of enserfment to individual lords for protection.

49. These estimates are presented in Q. Wright (1965), 656, 665, based on the work of Pitirim Sorokin. The total war casualties for all Europe, including World War I, were over 36 million; between 1500 and 1900, it was about 13 million. For western European nations, the total was over 7 million before 1900, and 20 million including World War I. See also Clodfelter (1992). Other large-scale killings that were more clearly regarded as political or politically related include

1600 and 1900. Thus wartime murder, rape, pillage, and starvation of other Europeans was seen to be acceptable; it was only their enslavement that was not.

Even Rousseau, who argued against any form of slavery, accepted "the right to kill its defenders [an Enemy State] as long as they bear arms," if it were a just war.[50] Enslavement, however, even of European war captives, was to be forbidden to Europeans. This European case was, of course, not the only intraracial or intranational examples of large-scale deaths. There were such cases of large numbers of deaths in nineteenth- and twentieth-century China and in the twentieth-century Soviet Union and Germany. Within Africa over the past half century, deaths in civil wars and related disputes now probably total above 15 million.[51] Wars and military actions have been large disrupters of world society, and wars and civil wars between non-racially distinct groups have had responsibility for considerable numbers of deaths.

IV

With this description of the world of slavery in which the U.S. South existed, I want now to describe some aspects of slavery in the Americas, partly to present some points of interest and partly to develop a context for the discussions of emancipation

---

the Nazi Holocaust, the Russian and Chinese revolutions, the Chinese Famine of 1959–61, the Taipei Rebellion, and the Mongol expansion led by Genghis Khan. Khan was probably responsible for the deaths of a larger percentage of the world's population at the time than any ruler. More dramatic in terms of relative population decline are the impact of the Black Death in Eurasia and the demographic disaster that hit the Native Americans with the expansion of Europe.

50. Rousseau (1997), 44–48. He goes on to argue that "one has the right to kill the enemy only when one cannot make him a slave," as a just war permits killing and/or enslavement.

51. See Engerman (forthcoming).

and the rise of free labor to be covered in the next chapters. In the initial settling of the Americas, including the thirteen colonies, slavery did not immediately play a major role. This came only several years after the arrival of Columbus and the coming of white settlers.[52] Slavery had existed in many parts of the Americas before Columbus, in most Native American societies, including the two largest, the Aztecs and the Incas, who accounted for over three-quarters of the Native American population circa 1500.[53] Among the Europeans, Spain was first to come to the Americas, and given the ability to decide where to settle, they went where the money and the Native American population were—following the Willie Sutton rule of colonial settlement. The Spanish and the Portuguese had about a one-century lead over the British, French, and Dutch. The latter nations were forced to locate in areas considered less desirable. The Spanish ending of Indian slavery came with the moral writings of Las Casas, but Spanish political and economic power meant that other means of coercion—some resembling those earlier practiced by Native Americans—were usable to obtain the desired labor force. In Brazil, the Portuguese had made some extensive use of Indian slave labor for sugar production, but over time (some seventy years), the relative price and production pat-

52. Columbus, after his first voyages, did send back slaves to Spain, but this was apparently "in total disregard of royal policy," and they were set free by the queen. See Phillips and Phillips (1992), 232. Indigenous slavery was declared illegal by the crown in 1542, but other means of labor coercion were permitted, as was the continued enslavement of black Africans. Following various forms of legislation against Indian slavery after 1570, Portuguese Brazil abolished Indian slavery in 1758. See Lockhart and Schwartz (1983), 266, 269, 282–85, and Haring (1947), 50–54.

53. See Denevan (1976), 289–92. On the migration patterns of Europeans and Africans, see Eltis (1983) and Eltis (2000), 9–10.

tern led to a shift from Indian slaves to African slaves. Thus, in Latin America, the Brazilian labor force became predominantly black African, and in the Spanish colonies, the labor force was predominantly Indian.[54] North America (meaning here the U.S. and Canada) and the Caribbean had relatively few Native Americans and, based on the needs dictated by climate and crops, drew upon different sources than did Spanish America for the desired labor force.[55]

Even after the British came to the Americas, their first major areas of settlement were in the Caribbean islands, not mainland North America, and settlement was on the basis of white labor, often indentured, which preceded the large-scale arrival of African slaves by some thirty to fifty years. The islands contained only a limited number of Native Americans. When, after 1690, the British shifted settlement to the thirteen mainland colonies, it still took several decades before slavery became quantitatively important there, and then in only some of the colonies. There were attempts to use Indian slave labor, whether purchased or captured, as the basis of the colonial labor system, particularly in South Carolina. However, most of the slaves from South Carolina and Spanish Florida were not for use in the area of acquisition but were sold elsewhere in the colonies. Indian slave labor, however, was relatively soon replaced by white labor in the North and slave labor in the South.[56] Four colonies made enslavement of Indians illegal by the mid-eighteenth century, but in the others, the question of legality did not affect its decline.[57] Thus, for Spain, Britain, and others, slavery was not si-

54. See Lockhart and Schwartz (1983), 194–201.

55. For a survey of settlement patterns, see most recently, Engerman and Sokoloff (2002).

56. Gallay (2002), 288–314.

57. Lauber (1913), 283–319. Several different explanations have been given for

multaneous with colonization. It took several decades before the colonies were able to develop the systematic set of production methods and institutions that permitted slavery to be socially profitable and generally acceptable to the Europeans.[58]

In the years from the end of the seventeenth century until the geographic expansion of slaves on the mainland for the cotton kingdom in the early nineteenth century, there were some rather dramatic changes in southern slavery. The period of the cotton kingdom, the most studied years of southern slavery, accounts for only about one-quarter of the time that slavery existed in the South. Slavery in the nineteenth century was dramatically different in many ways from the earlier three-quarters of its presence. The earlier focus on rice and tobacco was replaced by cotton as the primary crop grown by slave labor.[59] There was an extensive geographic spread from the eastern seaboard states, where almost all of the slaves had been before 1790, to the newer, more western, states, where by 1860 more than half the slaves were located. And this type of geographic relocation was to occur several decades later in Cuba and in Brazil. The relative decline of tobacco and the rise of cotton also meant an increased size of producing units. This suggests that the slave economy was rather adaptable to innovations in transport and production, such as the cotton gin, canals, the steamboat, and the railroad, and was able to benefit from various technical and organizational innovations.[60] The psychological and cultural

the relative decline of Indian slavery. Some argue that it was due to the difficulties of trying to enslave people near their homes, weakening control; others refer to the relative agricultural skills and development of Indians and blacks. See, for example, Lauber (1913), 287–302.

58. See Galenson (1981) and Eltis (2000).

59. See the export data in Shepherd and Walton (1972).

60. See, for example, Fogel (1989), 17–113; North (1961); and Lakwete (2003).

adjustment of the slave population to these changes, particularly to interstate movement, with its effects on the family and
kinship patterns, still remain to be studied in detail, but we do
know that slave owners seemed able to maintain their wealth
and political power despite, or more likely because of, the many
transformations.[61]

In the late antebellum era, slavery was clearly profitable to
slave owners. There had been great increases in cotton production, and judging by the rising price of slaves, the comments
by slave traders, slave owners, and the antislavery North, and
the continued willingness of northerners to lend to southerners,
the expectation throughout the nation was that the southern
slave economy could persist for a long time. The South may have
had limited industry and urbanization relative to the North, but
this was so only relative to industrialization in western Europe
and the northern states, a small part of the rest of the world.
The South's economic structure reflected in large measure the
changing profits of cotton agriculture, as seen in cyclical movements of the region's resources into and out of industry and urban areas as the cotton market developed. Structural economic
change in the North did not develop until after 1820, meaning
that any southern lag was only a relatively recent development,
not yet widely diffused and still a somewhat uncertain phenomenon.[62] While some debated the political implications of these

61. On the demographic impacts of this early geographic mobility, see Kulikoff (1983). See also Berlin (1998).

62. On the question of industrialization in the South, see Fogel (1989), 102–13.
There now seems rather limited disagreement on the profitability of slavery (at
least in the short run), on the relative levels of southern per capita incomes as
conventionally measured, on the degree of white literacy and voting within the
South, and the role of agricultural productivity in generating these differences.
Most arguments suggest that the failure to industrialize would become costly

structural changes and argued which economy was more sus-
ceptible to cyclical distress, many of the projections made at the
time did not ignore the current political and economic impact
of large and growing profits from cotton production.[63] The failures of the South, however costly they might seem, would be
expected to become consequential in ending the system only in
the future, an aspect of timing which should influence discussions of the causes of the Civil War, as well as help explain the
extended length of the military conflict.

Various projections of the expected time span before slavery's decline, when masters would be willing to free the slaves
voluntarily on economic grounds, were made in the antebellum period. They were generally based on looking at changing
land-labor ratios. Most pointed to a gradual and delayed process. Whatever the questions today about the so-called Nieboer-
Domar model, attention to land-labor ratios were central to antebellum debates on the persistence of slavery and also, as we
shall see, to arguments about what would happen with emancipation and to discussions of what would be the fortunes of
free labor. The University of Virginia economist George Tucker
had the most specific empirical argument about the decline of

only sometime in the future, certainly in a time span going beyond the onset of
the Civil War. For a related argument, see Starobin (1970), 189, who argues that
"the time when slavery would be absolutely detrimental to southern industries
remained quite far off." It is not clear when the South would pay the price of its
failure to make these adjustments, how severe were these costs in shortening the
Civil War, or to what extent current perceptions run together the antebellum
and postbellum periods. For relevant U.S. labor force data, see Lebergott (1964).
For a contemporary discussion (comparing the U.S. South and North) of the
economic advantage of slave labor, by Edward Gibbon Wakefield, see Drescher
(2002), 56–59. See also G. Wright (1978).

63. See, for example, the discussions of the differential behavior in the cyclical

slavery, basing the time of slave emancipation on comparing an adjusted land-labor ratio for the South with the land-labor ratio when serfdom ended in England.[64] Based on the 1840 census, he gave slavery some sixty to eighty years; later, based on the 1850 census, and after the addition of Texas, he projected a longer time period. This was quite optimistic (for antislavery advocates) relative to the projection by William Wilberforce concerning the argument that ending the British slave trade would lead to the peaceful and nonconflicted ending of slavery in the British colonies. Wilberforce estimated the expected lag between the end of the slave trade in 1808 and the ending of slavery to be at over two hundred years, and that only if no new lands were added to the British islands.[65]

Probably the most interesting of these projections, part of a rather complex discussion of the economic path of southern slavery, was by Abraham Lincoln, in the debates with Stephen Douglas in 1858.[66] Lincoln accepted that slavery had recently been in a "state of progress" but argued that slavery would "turn towards ultimate extinction," although this would not occur "in a day, nor in a year, nor in two years." Indeed his best estimate here seems to be not "less than a hundred years at the least," but

---

downturn of 1857, which hit the North more severely than it did the South. For some contemporary discussions, see Nevins (1950), 176–97.

64. Tucker (1855), 108–18, App. 28. For more on Tucker's analysis, see Fox-Genovese and Genovese (2005), 317.

65. Wilberforce (1807).

66. Lincoln (1989a), 514–15, 677–78, 807–11. Lincoln (677–78) did note "that it will occur in the best way for both races in God's own good time." Douglas (753) followed the logic of Lincoln's reliance on the theory of diminishing returns to note that his means of putting slavery on the way to "ultimate extinction" was to "hem them in until starvation seizes them," and by starving them to death, thus "extinguishing the [N]egro race."

only if slavery were prohibited from the territories and if no innovations such as the cotton gin, which delayed the timetable
of the founding fathers, occurred to extend the economic life
of slavery. Lincoln's argument was similar to that of Cairnes,
who claimed that it was probable that slavery would not end on
economic grounds for the foreseeable future. There were other
leading political figures, such as Horace Greeley, whose forecasts were similar to Lincoln's, about one hundred years to slavery's demise, consistent with what was known about rising slave
prices and increased southern cotton output and sales in the
world market.[67]

V

There is one aspect in which slavery in the United States has
been unique for a slave society, indeed completely different from
the behavior of most other nations, free or slave, at the time—
the demographic experience. Starting in the eighteenth century
and up to the end of slavery (and probably also after freedom, at
least until 1880), the slave population grew at an unusually rapid
rate, about as high as that for U.S. whites.[68] For a slave society
this was a most unexpected occurrence, since elsewhere, in the
Americas and in the ancient world, slave populations were not
able to reproduce themselves. In the Americas outside of the
United States, the large numbers of imported slaves exceeded
the magnitude of the surviving slave population in the early
nineteenth century. Thus what was most striking about the U.S.
slave population and distinguished the United States from other

67. See, for example, on Greeley, Van Deusen (1958), 90–92, and also Bushnell's
(1860, 11) forecast, in November of 1860, of "no more than about seventy-five or
a hundred years." This, he argues, would occur whether slavery is in decline or
growing rapidly.

68. See Fogel (1989), 114–53.

slave areas was its exceptionally high rate of fertility, about as high as that for southern whites, which reduced the need for more imported slaves from Africa to maintain population totals, unlike the cases of the West Indies and Brazil.

These demographic aspects have led to debates about their implications concerning the treatment of slaves, the possible interferences with slave fertility, and the nature of cultural adaptations (such as marriage patterns and lactation periods), as well as concerning contemporary and later problems with the black family. It has also raised important issues of cultural interest for the study of the slave population. The high share of those native-born in the slave population in the United States relative to elsewhere in the Americas is important for analyzing differences in slave culture, the nature of slave revolts and resistance, and the question of African survivals, since survivals would be expected to be greater in places such as Brazil and Cuba, where the slave trade with Africa continued longer and where more of the slave population was African-born, compared to the United States.[69]

The higher ratio of the share of creoles in the U.S. slave population meant a more equal sex ratio, and thus the possibility of more stable family structure than in areas where there was a flow of predominantly male newcomers in the slave trade, with a general 60–40 male-female ratio, and where patterns of slave mortality made long-term stability more difficult. Thus the unusual demographic pattern of the U.S. slaves raises important issues, both for understanding the slave experience and for the study of developments after emancipation.

69. See Fogel (1989), 154–98, and Fogel (2003). As Richard Price (1973), 29–39, has pointed out, the interpretation of African survivals in the New World is difficult, since African societies were very dynamic internally and we might expect

I do want to add a further point about the measure of material treatment of the slaves, since it permits the use of some relatively interesting data and concepts, which are consistent with other forms of historical evidence that have been widely used. The relatively greater height of slaves in the United States compared to those in the West Indies and to Africans is a pattern that suggests that it was some combination of better nutrition, lesser work demands, and a more favorable disease environment that influenced the demographic differences between U.S. and Caribbean slaves.[70] Nevertheless, the issue of material treatment has little, if anything, to do with the morality of slavery. As Frederick Douglass commented in describing the evils of slavery: "My feelings were not the result of any marked cruelty in the treatment I received; they sprung from the consideration of my being a slave at all. . . . The feeding and clothing me well, could not atone for taking my liberty from me."[71] A similar point was made later by the British socialist R. H. Tawney, who linked his criticism of slavery to one of the proslavery claims. He repeated a familiar argument that there was possibly a higher level of food and other material consumption among slaves than among British workers, but he claims that this is not relevant to the antislavery argument since the big point was the loss of freedom.[72] Nevertheless, the questions of material

---

changes to occur in African New World societies which, he argues, would be consistent with the nature of "deeper" African patterns.

70. See Fogel (1989), 138–47, drawing, in part, from the work of Richard Steckel.

71. Douglass (1969), 161.

72. Tawney (1972), 12. "And this feeling against slavery, be it noted, is quite independent of whether a man treats his slaves kindly or not. However kind a slave owner might be—and he might be much kinder than many English

treatment discussed by Douglass, even if not relevant for judging the morality of slavery, are important for understanding the lives of the slaves and for evaluating the background to their adjustment to freedom.

---

businesses—he is condemned because he is outraging the deepest human sentiment, the sentiment which forbids a human being to be treated as a thing in law." The same point was made earlier in the English Civil War debates, as paraphrased by Skinner (2002), 27: "An absolute ruler may choose to enrich instead of kill you, but you are none the less a slave for that. What takes away your liberty is the mere fact of living at the mercy of someone else," and "it is all too easy to live in servitude without suffering actual oppression or constraint."

Two

EMANCIPATION IN WORLD PERSPECTIVE

THERE ARE TWO GENERAL issues about emancipation that will be considered: first, how it was accomplished and, second, what were its effects. In regard to the first, the United States, with uncompensated emancipation, was unusual among the major New World slave societies, even areas in the Americas with relatively few slaves. The ending of slavery in the United States was also atypical compared with most of the rest of the world and also compared with the payment schemes attending the end of serfdom in Europe. In the New World, emancipation did not come about due to economic decay and a voluntary freeing of slaves by owners. Rather, it came about via peacetime government legislation in almost all cases, except in Saint Domingue, where it resulted from a slave revolt, and in the United States, where military action led to legislation. Outside of the United States, emancipation generally came with some form of compensation given to slave owners—in the form of cash or bonds (paid for by the taxpayers) or labor time, with the "free womb" provision and apprenticeship enforcing labor as a form of compensation (paid for, in effect, by the slaves).[1] Emancipation generally was gradual, not immediate, taking in some cases more than a quarter century after the initial legislation. Haiti, where the slaves achieved their freedom by revolution, later agreed (in 1825) to pay compensation intended for the former slave

1. For an estimation of the breakdown of costs permitting an estimate of the value of the free womb provision, see Fogel and Engerman (1974b).

owners in France, as a condition for entering into trading relations with the French. This compensation was actually paid to France, but it is still unclear if it got to the appropriate former slave owners.[2]

The U.S. slaveholders received no compensation of any form after the Civil War, although some schemes had been discussed before the war. During the war, compensation at a low price was paid to slave owners in Washington, and Lincoln claimed some form of compensation would be cheaper than the financial costs of fighting the war.[3] The southern slave owners lost their slaves, thus the market value of these assets. While they lost the gross output of slave labor, they no longer had to pay for the maintenance or consumption of the ex-slaves, and were thus freed from the obligation to support children. If slavery had been unprofitable, with maintenance costs exceeding slave output, ending slavery could have been a financial benefit to slaveholders. U.S. slave owners, like former slave owners elsewhere (except Haiti), however, were able to keep their land and capital, although the ending of slavery reduced the value of land and other assets. Emancipation ended enslavement, as in Europe it ended serfdom, but in both of these cases policies were limited in their impact on the distribution of wealth and political power. And, perhaps surprising to current sensibilities, in no case were

2. See, e.g., Rotberg (1971).

3. See Fladeland (1976) and Lincoln (1989b), 310–11, 393–415. In March 1862, Lincoln contrasted the costs of emancipation to slave owners in the Union states (at below market prices, however) with the costs per day of the war (financial, excluding deaths), 310–11, 409, arguing that the former would "shorten the war" and be more "prudent and economical." His proposal was for a gradual emancipation with compensation in the form of bonds. The trade-off was $400 per slave for eighty-seven days of war. To pay compensation at market prices for all U.S. slaves in 1860, the federal budget would have increased by about fifty times and the payment in annual interest if bonds were issued would at least triple the budget.

the ex-slaves or ex-serfs provided with compensation or reparations for their previous exploitation.

The nineteenth-century freeing of serfs in Russia did have some unexpected effects. Thaddeus Stevens, the antislavery representative from Pennsylvania and a leading Radical Republican, regarded the failure to provide "forty acres and a mule" to ex-slaves as meaning that they received fewer gains relative to the Russian serfs, since former serfs were able to obtain some land.[4] Yet, on closer examination, it appears that the Russian terms suggest that the ex-serfs paid an above-market price for the land, thus actually getting a negative financial return from emancipation. In addition, there were much greater constraints on individual and family mobility, and these persisted for a considerably longer time in Russia than in the United States.[5]

In discussing slave emancipation, it is useful to distinguish the freeing of individuals or families by manumission by owners and the freeing of all slaves by some form of legislation. Individual manumissions were a general feature of most slave societies. It was sometimes given as a gift provided by the owners, but possibly more frequently, manumission was a grant to the slave of the right to purchase him- or herself with money that the slave could earn to be used for this purpose. Manumission was generally seen, from Greek times forward, as a device to help maintain the system of slavery, part of a set of arrangements for owners to maintain control and provide an incentive for productive slave labor and good behavior.[6] Its limited nature

4. See Trefousse (1997), 210–23.

5. See Domar (1989). For details on the Russian emancipation debates, see Kingston-Mann (1999) and Field (1976). See also Kolchin (1987) and Moon (2001) on the Russian reaction to emancipation.

6. See Patterson (1982), 262–96. See also Aristotle (cited in Wiedemann, 1981, 185–86.) The role of manumission as incentive, or as safety valve, is described by

was not seen as a threat to the system, and the numbers of freed ex-slaves tended to be small in most societies.[7] While to some the greater ability to become manumitted was regarded as a sign of a more open slave society, it should be noted that those New World areas in which manumission had been most frequent, the Spanish and Portuguese settlements, were the last areas of the New World to end slavery as a labor system.[8]

Little is known in detail about the ending of slavery in most premodern societies. Although slave societies often included detailed rules and laws about who could be enslaved and how they could be treated and manumitted, there is little evidence about any legislation regarding the process of overall emancipation or even if emancipation was based on some specific legislation.[9] It often appears that slavery simply faded away and was no longer enforced by governments and slave owners, as in twentieth-century Africa. It is this lack of clarity that makes dating the precise ending of slavery difficult.

In explaining his view of the expiration of Roman slavery and the movement from slave groups to small, family farms,

(Pseudo-) Aristotle (1935), 339: "Every slave should have before his eyes a definite goal or term of his labor. To set the prize of freedom before him is both just and expedient; since having a prize to work for, and a time defined for its attainment, he will put his heart into his labors." For a more recent variant, note the reward structure described by Craton (1978), 222. For discussions of manumission in other times and places, see, for example, Jordan (1986), Schafer (2003), and the Siete Partidas (Burns, 2001).

7. See McGlynn (1989) for essays on patterns of manumission in several different areas.

8. For the comparison of manumission patterns in Iberian and northwestern European colonies, see Tannenbaum (1946).

9. See Karras (1988) for an excellent discussion of this issue in Scandinavia and elsewhere in Europe.

Moses Finley argues for the role of increased population and the loss of external markets in driving the value of the slave's surplus (production above consumption) to zero.[10] Freedom occurred when the entire population's productivity was at subsistence, and, in effect, all workers could become free but at subsistence incomes.

Another mechanism for ending a system of coerced labor, which explains the end of serfdom in England but could in principle be applicable to slavery, occurred when the Black Death in the fourteenth century reduced the population of laborers in Europe, while the amount of productive land was unchanged, making for a labor shortage.[11] In some cases, such as in eastern Europe, labor scarcity led to a tightened serfdom, but in fourteenth-century England the cartel of serf-users fell apart, and there developed competitive bidding among the landowners for laborers, bidding up labor incomes as well as providing such nonpecuniary benefits as freedom. This case demonstrates the great importance of slave owners as a group not allowing people to try to attract slaves away from their owners and the need to respect each other's property rights by strictly enforcing laws regarding ownership rights.

Another early ending of a form of slavery, based less on economic than political reasons, was the case of the Scottish coal miners, discussed by Adam Smith. The miners had binding contracts that precluded mobility. Initially based on a law of 1606,

10. Finley (1998), 191–217. According to Finley, rural workers were "steadily being depressed into . . . dependency, of unfreedom" (215). This argument, that slavery can end when all are "unfree," is consistent with Domar (1970).

11. This process is described in Hilton (1969). The reduction in the English population in 1348–1349 was estimated to be between 30 and 45 percent. See Hatcher (1977), 25.

in reaction to a shortage of workers in the industry, this system was not legally ended until 1799.[12] This ending, both because of the small numbers involved and because it seemed to be regarded more as serfdom than slavery, did not attract much attention, then or now.

For the eighteenth and nineteenth centuries, the legal dating of the end of slavery is more clear-cut. Modern slavery was first ended in the Americas by settlers from western Europe and their descendants, and only later did emancipation spread to their other colonies and then to independent nations in Asia and Africa. It is striking that, within a period of only about one century after the start of the first antislavery movement in England, slavery was ended in the Americas and, in the same century, serfdom abolished in Europe, and that it was then, over the next three-quarters of a century, ended as a legal institution in various colonies and other European offshoots, and in much of the world. While we often treat the subject of emancipation as a distinct process for each nation, the similarity in timing, in arguments, and in policies suggests the usefulness of examining a broader European and American pattern, not just the country-specific factors usually stressed. Emancipations in Asia and Africa, though belated, were generally accomplished under the influence of European ideas and political power. Nevertheless, other forms of coerced labor organization continue to exist to the present day, and even slavery of a traditional form seems to have remained in parts of Africa.

While most slave societies (including Western, Islamic, and Asian societies) had argued that slaves should be treated well and that individual manumissions were a desirable thing, the

12. See Smith (1978), 1:191–92; A. Campbell (1979); Whatley (2000).

idea of an attack on slavery as a system and a willingness to end it was a much later development. While all religions had advocated kind treatment of slaves, it was only later, and in Christian areas, that an attack on the system was begun. Slave revolts, when they did occur, have been argued to have an indirect impact on ending slavery, but it was only in Saint Domingue that revolt had a direct effect on the ending of the system, forcing a complete change in the structure of political power.

II

Modern emancipations have several characteristics in common that merit examination. At the time of the ending of slavery and serfdom, all European societies had a firm belief in the sanctity of property rights (by nonslaves), and the need to compensate for property actually taken away from individuals. As seen in earlier arguments concerning compensation at the end of the British slave trade, however, there could be key arguments against compensation that were interesting politically and which do raise questions about maintaining property rights. As William Pitt, the Younger, argued in the debate concerning the ending of the slave trade, such a policy of making illegal the owning of an asset requiring compensation paid by the government would not only be expensive but would be difficult for the government to implement. Some argued that anyone dealing with a government knows the government could always change policy; others argued that if a government were required to pay compensation for any policy change, it would be impossible to have anything change.[13] Despite these negative arguments, how-

13. See Burke in Cobbett (1816), 96–97, and Pitt in Cobbett (1817), 145–46. Similar arguments still exist today, but in many cases today there seems little concern about those individuals who are losing.

ever, in almost all cases of ending slavery and serfdom in the nineteenth century, compensation was paid to slave owners and serf owners, reducing their losses from freeing the slaves. While they lost direct legal control of labor, they seldom lost their land (or political power). In ending serfdom, moreover, owners were often given land taken from the serfs or were able to purchase their land at a low price. Such compensation to slave owners and serf users was not always in full, since it was often a product of negotiations, bargained about as part of the legislative process, but it did serve to reduce somewhat the magnitude of the capital loss imposed by emancipation.[14]

Most of the slave societies in the Americas (and elsewhere), including the colonies of England, France, the Netherlands, Denmark, Spain, and Portugal, had first ended the international slave trade some twenty-five to fifty years prior to their ending slavery.[15] In part, this was because it was presumably easier to attack the purchase of people moved long distances from their homes, via a long voyage, than it was to attack slavery as an ongoing social system of human interactions in a given area. When the movement to end the slave trade began, the British aboli-

14. See Fogel and Engerman (1974b). Part of the bargaining concerning the compensation amount was the determination of the date for which market prices would be applied. In no case was compensation paid for the reduced land prices resulting from slave emancipation. There were debates in Parliament about what years should be used to determine slave prices for compensation and whether payment should be based on slave prices or slave numbers.

15. See Engerman (1995). The last two to end slavery in the New World came long after the ending of the legal slave trade, thirty-seven years after the arrival of the last slave in the international slave trade in the case of Brazil, but only nineteen years in the case of Cuba. These were seventeen years after the first emancipation law for Brazil and sixteen years for Cuba.

tionists were clear to state for political reasons that they were not attacking slavery, only the transatlantic movement of people. It was, however, sometimes argued that ending the slave trade would end slavery. This could be for two possible, quite different reasons, both of which provided long-term examples of gradual emancipation. One, drawing upon the demographic knowledge of the natural decrease of the West Indian slave population, posited gradual emancipation via demographic attrition, arguing that with no new inflow the slave population would ultimately disappear, ending slavery without need of a legally passed emancipation. (This was not to be an immediate event, however, since, as noted above, Wilberforce placed the time for this to occur at over two hundred years.) Second, it was argued that the reduction in the number of slaves would make them more valuable and thus lead to a policy of amelioration and better treatment by their owners, with better treatment ultimately meaning free labor.[16] In the British Caribbean, for which these two arguments were both made, neither, of course, occurred, and about one-quarter century after legislatively ending the slave trade, Parliament abolished slavery itself. It might be noted that, despite their pleas in 1807, no compensation was paid to any British transatlantic slave traders for the capital loss on their specialized vessels and equipment. The British compensated only those vessels that were at sea at the time the legislation was passed, and had thus incurred actual expenses to acquire trading goods.[17]

16. See the discussion in Wilberforce (1807). For a similar argument applied to the U.S., see Cairnes (1969), 350, who claims that with a reduction in the available labor supply "the life of the slave would become for his master an object of increased consideration; his comfort would be more attended to, and his condition would rapidly improve," until emancipation was achieved.

17. See Porter (1970).

Compensation could take several forms. Owners could be paid in cash, in bonds, or in labor time. The government cash and bond payments were generally set, in total, by legislation, and they were sometimes divided among individuals on the basis of observed slave prices, allowing for the age and gender composition of the slave labor force. In these cases, the ultimate burden of the costs of emancipation was borne by taxpayers. The compensation in the form of labor time was accomplished in two ways. One was to legislate a set time for adult slaves to keep working for their owners, under laboring conditions similar to those under slavery. Such a system of apprenticeship was used by the British (four to six years) and, later, by the Dutch (ten years). The alternative method, and by far the most frequent manner of ending slavery in the Americas and elsewhere, was called, when introduced in Brazil in 1871, the law of the free womb. This meant that only those born after a specified date were to be considered free and that, though they were considered not to be slaves, they were required to work for the owner of their mothers for some period of time, usually fifteen to thirty years, depending on the countries, and, in some cases, differentiated by sex. In several cases, the passage of the law of the free womb was followed, after some years, by a general emancipation of those enslaved and of those legally free but bound into apprenticeship. This, however, did not occur either in the northern states of the United States or in most of South America until after a period of years, ranging from twenty to sixty in the former (with one case, Pennsylvania, never legislatively ending slavery) and twenty to forty years in the latter. Thus much of the decline in slavery in the Americas was due to the deaths of those earlier enslaved, relatively few of whom would ultimately have benefited from freedom, and not to the legal freeing of individual slaves.

As mentioned, the law of the free womb presented several advantages for slave owners and for other free people in society. Such a scheme meant, in effect, that slaves were paying for their own freedom by working for masters and providing them with surplus output once they became productive in their teens and twenties after paying for their own costs of raising themselves. This meant that taxpayers were saved from paying for the full costs of emancipation, since the freeborn were eventually earning enough to pay for the expenses of raising themselves. Emancipation was thus made more politically feasible and acceptable, since taxpayers did not need to worry about paying the compensation.[18] During this apprenticeship period, moreover, the freeborn would be laboring under supervisors and thus receive some "education" that would, hopefully, permit them to deal more successfully as members of a free society.

The law of the free womb was the common means of achieving a gradual emancipation, although immediate emancipation would seem to have been the obvious and most moral way to end this system of robbery and theft, as slavery was often described, and of providing the benefits of freedom to people as rapidly as possible. The belief in the need to educate slaves for freedom, however, poses important questions for the design of policy, as gradual emancipation was not regarded only

18. See Fogel and Engerman (1974b). A similar calculation was made by Frances Hutcheson (1968), 2:81–85, who claimed "it would generally be found that the labors of any person sound in body and mind, would sufficiently discharge this debt [the expenses of his maintenance in his childhood] before he came to thirty years of age; and where there were any considerable dexterity, they would discharge it much sooner." Hutcheson was concerned with the claims upon children of slaves, and he further argued that it was when they "attain to the age of ten or twelve, when their labors begin to compensate their maintenance," an age roughly similar to that in the U.S. South prior to the Civil War.

as a mechanism to add to labor time, which had the effects of compensating slave owners and avoided burdening taxpayers. Quobna Ottobah Cugoano, an African former slave, writing in 1787, argued that there should be "a universal emancipation of slaves," but it would be immediate only for "those who had been above seven years in the islands or elsewhere, if they have obtained any competent degree of knowledge of the Christian religion, and the laws of civilization, and had behaved themselves honestly and decently." He argued that slavery was robbery, but he considered the seven years from the date of arrival in the islands as the period to make "suitable progress in knowledge" and to "become tractable and obedient, useful laborers, dutiful servants and good subjects." Another benefit of the seven-year period, pointed to by Cugano, was that it would be sufficient to repay former slaves' owners for the "expences attending their education."[19] Thus the introduction of the British period of apprenticeship with stipendiary magistrates and the U.S. creation of the Freedmen's Bureau to aid the ex-slaves during the transition period were meant to solve the problem of preparing people for freedom, although it is now argued by many that both did more to help the ex-slaves' former owners than they did to help the ex-slaves. These institutions did face a particular tension, however, given the nature of the antislavery argument. For if one of the evils of slavery was that it permitted the life of an individual to be controlled by another, then to liberate people only to have them become wards to be controlled by the state

19. Cugoano (1999), 98–99. Cugoano's gradualism may be surprising, given his frequent description of slavery as "robbery and theft" (57–59). Many antislavery societies in different countries made similar arguments for the desirability of some form of gradual emancipation, since slaves were not yet ready, economically or socially, for freedom. See also Nash (1990), 13, 15, 20, 43–49, 146–58.

or other individuals would seem a somewhat contradictory and unacceptable policy.

The case for gradual emancipation was made many times in the nineteenth century, with the implications that only at the end of some set period of time would the ex-slaves be able to satisfactorily function as free people within society. This belief followed from the abolitionist position that it was the slave status and the treatment within it, not their biological background, that had been limiting the slaves' accomplishments. This relation between the antislavery argument and the need for gradual emancipation had actually been expressed earlier by others, including two leading French philosophers of the seventeenth and eighteenth centuries—Bodin and Condorcet—who argued that, if slavery was as psychologically destructive to the slave as argued in the attack on slavery, then an immediate emancipation would leave the freedmen unable to develop the necessary skills to adapt at once to their new status. There was also a need for time to learn the necessary skills and this was to be aided by providing groups to aid the process of emancipation, such as the British stipendiary magistrates and the U.S. Freedmen's Bureau.[20]

Correspondingly, for those believing that immediate emancipation would be successful, there were certain implications to be drawn concerning the effects of slavery and the abilities of the slaves to deal with those conditions. In most major cases, except for Haiti, the United States, and the Danish and French

20. See Bodin (1962), 45–46, and Condorcet (1999), 313–15. The same argument for gradual emancipation, based on the "mental degradation" caused by slavery, was a frequently repeated theme in many societies. Some similar transition issues have emerged recently in the case of eastern Europe, with initial declines in output and concern with the readiness and/or ability of the population to adapt to a new form of economic organization; the delay in achieving successful adjustments does resemble that of the earlier cases of slave and serf emancipation.

Caribbean islands, emancipation in the Americas was a gradual process, often with a period of apprenticeship prior to full freedom. The key issues were determining for whom the apprentice would work, what their conditions of work would be, including the length of the workday, and who would adjudicate any disagreements between landlords and workers. In all cases, the apprentices were expected to work for their former owners, on the same producing units as before. Tocqueville, while conceding the need for apprenticeship, advocated—based on his belief about the negative psychological effects of master-slave interactions—a form of state ownership for continued production.[21] The legislation regarding apprenticeship in the British West Indies debated the number of weekly hours and the effect this decision had on the ability of apprentices to allocate time for working their own lands in addition to those of their former owners. When it was deemed necessary in the British West Indies to introduce legislation to control labor, the colonies generally reverted to the master and servant rules that had long been and were still being applied to regulate and discipline free white workers in England.[22]

21. See Tocqueville (1840). Also, Tocqueville (2003), 215–16, writing in 1843 after the British emancipation, argued that "the English government should thus have refused, at least for some time, to grant Negroes the right to acquire land; but it never had a very clear idea of the period when there was still time to avert it. At the moment when slavery was abolished, such a restriction of freedom would have been accepted without murmur by the black population; later it would be imprudent to impose it." The purpose was to prevent the freedmen from acquiring some of the great expanse of the available land, and thus becoming small landowners rather than simple wage workers, a restriction which he regarded as being most crucial for their future development.

22. On the Master and Servant Acts, see Steinfeld (1991, 2001) and Hay and Craven (2004). In 1848, Henry Barkly "claimed that the West Indian vagrancy

III

In general, most of the slave emancipations in the Americas had somewhat similar effects on ex-slave welfare and material income. The slaves appeared to have benefited from freedom and, economically, from some combination of increased leisure time, a lessened intensity of labor, and lowered labor force participation rates. This, however, was often at the expense of lowered output, particularly of export crops, but possibly also of the output produced for consumption of the ex-slaves. In general, emancipation meant a disappearance or at least relative decline of the plantation system, with labor shifting to work on small units, which were sometimes owned by or rented by ex-slaves, but also were frequently owned by whites who used ex-slaves as hired workers, at least initially. Since, in most cases, it appears that the still politically powerful planters would have preferred to continue plantation production even with free labor, the economic, political, and moral constraints that prevented the return to the full coercion of labor on plantations is still unclear. While the political balance of power was clearly with the ruling class, its members accepted limits upon what they could do to reimpose a plantation economy. Haiti, moreover, was no more successful in reintroducing a plantation system than were most European colonies.

In most cases, per capita output of the slave society fell with emancipation, a decline that sometimes persisted but could, as in the case of the United States, reverse itself relatively quickly

---

laws were no different from that of England," since the colonists had mainly copied the laws that they had known in England. See Engerman (1996), 3. These British acts did discriminate by class, if not by race, and included what may then and now still be considered to be slavelike conditions. See Steinfeld (2001) on the degrees of coercion in so-called free labor markets.

and then lead to the onset of rapid economic growth. In the context of quite common declines in output after emancipation, those cases without a decline or with a relatively rapid reversal were explained either by high population densities (for example, Barbados) or by the subsequent development of a new labor force, often from foreign lands (for example, British Guiana and Trinidad), to produce plantation crops.

Variations in responses in different areas were often based upon differences in land-labor ratios and the quality of the soil available for production. Since most colonial societies introduced similar legislation to control ex-slave labor, in an attempt to limit geographic mobility and force plantation labor, the various adjustments that took place reflected more the nature of resource endowments than legislative intent. In the British areas, for example, all colonies aimed at restricting labor mobility by using, in effect, the British Master and Servant Acts, but this policy was effective only when there was limited land available relative to the labor supply, as in Barbados and Antigua. If land was abundant, as in Trinidad and British Guiana, the desired policies were often ineffective, and other measures, such as the introduction of indentured servitude, would ultimately be necessary to permit economic expansion. In cases such as Jamaica, however, the population density was too low to maintain the plantation system, but the soil did not permit competition with the newer colonies of Trinidad and British Guiana, and long-term stagnation emerged.

The diverse patterns of adjustments to emancipation in the New World demonstrate the economic and political adaptability in these areas, adaptability that had, no doubt, also existed under slavery. In Haiti, the response to emancipation was the most extreme of all. Early attempts to reintroduce a plantation regime producing sugar for the world market were not successful.[23] The freed population wished to avoid working on sugar production, and they could not be forced into this by the power of government. Ultimately, in the twentieth century, Haiti suffered the great tragedy of not only becoming the lowest income nation in the Americas but, with the migration of Haitian labor, becoming an important part of the labor force in the production of plantation sugar in both Cuba and the Dominican Republic.[24] The economic and political difficulties of Haiti were examined after its successful revolution, both by proslavery and antislavery advocates. The former argued that the economic and political problems observed there were the inevitable results of freeing blacks, and the latter presented demographic and cultural arguments to argue that emancipation (even in Haiti, with its continued social and political disturbances) should be regarded as a success.

Three decades after Haitian independence, there occurred in the British West Indies the first major legislated emancipation in the Americas. There were three patterns of reaction. Barbados was regarded as the major success of emancipation, as it maintained a plantation system, had productive labor, and increased output immediately upon emancipation, and it continued to do so into the twentieth century. This success was due, mainly, to the limited land available relative to its population (before emigration began, first to islands in the Caribbean and later to the U.S.), not necessarily to the impact of legislation. This is suggested by the other case of increased output during emancipa-

23. See, among other useful sources, Dubois (2004a, b), Fass (1988), Leyburn (1941), Nicholls (1979), and Rotberg (1971).

24. Moreno Fraginals (1986). See Moya Pons (1995), 368–69. In October 1937, Trujillo's army assassinated somewhere between ten thousand and twenty thousand Haitians in Santo Domingo, but they did pay some compensation in 1939.

tion, Antigua, whose planters had voted against introducing the period of apprenticeship, since, they argued, the limited land available meant that freed slaves had no alternatives to doing the same work that they had done prior to freedom.[25]

The other cases of successful emancipation, at least as measured by increased sugar production in the long run (after about twenty to thirty years), were British Guiana and Trinidad, areas that had been expanding in the early nineteenth century under slavery, and Mauritius, which was able to introduce indentured labor from India immediately upon the ending of slavery.[26] In these cases, however, success required a revision in British legislation concerning international migration of indentured labor. This change, influencing Mauritius, British Guiana, and Trinidad, became effective almost immediately in Mauritius, but elsewhere it took almost a quarter century. In these cases labor inflows occurred mainly from India but also from China, the Portuguese Atlantic islands, and Africa, a movement of low-income workers for a five- or ten-year term of labor on the sugar plantations of the Americas.[27] The ex-slaves generally were able to avoid plantation labor, operating small farms in non-plantation areas of the colonies. The movements to British Guiana and Trinidad were not the only streams of movement of indentured labor, as some Indian workers went to the French and Dutch colonies in the Caribbean to produce sugar, the Dutch receiving laborers also from their East Indian colonies. Other indentured

25. See Engerman (1982, 1984). On Antigua, see the comments in the Antiguan legislature seeing no need for apprenticeship, as ex-slaves could work only on plantations because of the high labor-land ratio.

26. See, most recently, Laurence (1994) and Look Lai (1993).

27. For indentured labor more generally, see Northrup (1995), Tinker (1974), and Roberts and Byrne (1966).

workers went to produce sugar and other plantation commodi-
ties in Peru and South Africa (which earlier had had slavery),
and still others went to Australia and Fiji, areas without a prior
existence of settler-imposed slavery.[28]

The third category among the British colonies is illustrated
by Jamaica, whose sugar production declined with emancipation. Jamaica acquired some indentured labor, but because of
limited productivity of the soil, its use was unprofitable. Jamaica
and several other West Indian islands, which suffered permanent declines in sugar output and long-term declines in income,
became islands of small family farms in less productive parts of
the islands. Several decades later, Jamaica did experience some
economic recovery, on the basis of producing bananas for the
export market, but sugar never recovered its earlier position.[29]

Within these three quite different overall patterns in the
British West Indian colonies, there were some similarities to
note. Ex-slaves, when freed, chose to avoid plantation work and
became family farmers on small units, preferably farms they
owned. The major case in which this did not occur was Barbados, not because of different worker preferences but because,
as noted above, there was no free, available land on the island,
and it was several years before emigration was allowed. These
different outcomes did not reflect differences in the legislation
accompanying emancipation but were influenced to a great extent by the land and soil endowments in the various areas. Those
areas, such as Trinidad and British Guiana, in which, over time,
output increased were places where plantation labor was rein-
stated. The timing of the re-emergence of plantations in those

28. For general descriptions of sugar production and indentured labor, see also
Deerr (1949–1950).

29. See Hall (1959).

areas makes it more probable that, when indentured labor was important, it was because the ex-slaves had previously been able to avoid plantation labor. This made it necessary, if sugar production would be profitable and was desired, to attract labor, under some form of coercion, from elsewhere. It seems less probable that the labor from overseas was first induced to come, and that it then drove the ex-slaves out of sugar production. It is also doubtful that it was the arrival of indentured labor that drove out local labor from plantations in those societies that developed sugar production without previously having had slavery, such as Australia and Fiji, or where slavery had previously been of quite limited importance, such as the Dominican Republic.

The declining amount of ex-slave labor in the production of plantation crops and their replacement by new sources of labor also characterized some other areas. In these cases, differences and changes in technology played an important role. In cotton and coffee production, for which plantation operations were more efficient than were family farms, it was, however, possible for smaller units to produce for export, even with less efficiency and, probably, higher capital costs. Thus the ending of slavery in Brazil meant an ending of coffee production on plantations. However, coffee production was still quite feasible in Brazil after slavery ended; indeed the country remained the world's largest producer. But it maintained its position on the basis of a new labor force of small coffee-farmers attracted from southern Europe, primarily Italy, Spain, and Portugal, often with Brazilian governmental subsidies, including land grants.[30] In the United States, as we shall see in more detail, the decline of the cotton

30. See, for example, Holloway (1980). See also Clarence-Smith and Topik (2003), 31–33, 360–410, 422–23.

plantation as a production unit using slave labor was followed by a shift to small farms, of both black and white labor, to produce cotton. The major change allowed by this movement to smaller, less efficient cotton farms was that, whereas in 1860 white farms, as opposed to slave units, produced only about 10 percent of all cotton (and that in a year of high demand and profitability), by 1880 the southern white share of cotton production was about 60 percent. In the U.S. South, there was no need for foreign labor, as the cotton-producing labor force now came from white southerners who had been unable to compete with an economically successful plantation system in the antebellum period. Thus the attempts to introduce Chinese and Italian labor in the postbellum years became unnecessary.

The case of sugar is more complex, since under the earlier technology it was just about impossible (outside of Asia) to have small-scale production, and even that could not compete successfully with plantations.[31] In the late nineteenth century, technological developments, including improvements in railroads leading to faster delivery of the cane to the mill, permitted the introduction of central mills that allowed sugar to be produced on small farms. Part of Cuba's adjustment to the end of slavery included the expansion of central mills and cane farms, with the labor force being primarily white Spanish immigrants, whose travel was subsidized. Cuba maintained some production on sugar plantations, using black labor and later drawing some plantation labor from Jamaica and Haiti. The racial breakdown in sugar-producing units also characterized Louisiana, where

31. In India and China, small sugar farms existed before the end of world slavery, but they were generally for internal markets, not able to compete with slave plantations in export markets. For China, see Mazumdar (1998), and for India, see Deerr (1949–1950), 1:40–62.

whites owned and worked on cane farms and blacks worked on plantations.[32]

Although it had not had a slave system, mainly because of its relatively late date of settlement and the availability of convict labor from Britain, Australia is an interesting case to look at to see what the range of labor policy could be. Toward the end of the nineteenth century, Australia decided to undertake sugar production in Queensland. Consistent with its racism, the government brought in indentured laborers from various Pacific islands—the so-called blackbirders—for plantation labor. By the end of the century, however, still being racist, Australia ended the stream of Pacific Island labor inward and tried to compel those already there to return in order to achieve a "White Australia." Australians, however, still wanted domestic production of sugar, which they felt could be obtained from cane farms using mainly Italian workers. This could be successfully done only with a complex system of tariffs and bounties, which, while costly, was a price willingly paid (by some) to indulge their racist beliefs.[33] Thus the Australians were aware of the effect of their policies on the cost of sugar but were willing to pay it to achieve their particular aims. The British had, of course, realized this earlier, at the time of emancipation, when they tried, for a short time, to encourage desirable outcomes in their colonies by imposing higher tariffs on slave-produced sugar than on sugar pro-

32. On Louisiana, see Sitterson (1953) and Rodrigue (2001), and for Cuba, Scott (1985, 2005).

33. For a description of migration from the Pacific Islands to work in the Australian sugar industry, see Corris (1973) and Docker (1970). The discussion of the transition to white labor in sugar production is examined in Parliament of the Commonwealth of Australia (1912).

duced by free labor in the British Colonies.[34] If they had been successful, this would have provided benefits to the sugar-producing islands of the British West Indies, supporting the outcome of emancipation, but such an outcome was possible only by imposing higher costs on consumers. This policy, however, was soon reversed, and tariff differentials, based on the nature of the labor institutions producing sugar, were ended by 1854.

IV

Having completed this brief survey of emancipations and described some common patterns, I shall now describe the U.S. case in more detail. In some ways—the decline in output and the end of the plantation system—the South resembled the other cases of emancipation, suggestive of some very important aspects of slavery as a system of labor control, as well as why slavery was introduced and what happened when it ended. It provides some understanding of the preferences of people regarding living and working conditions that were to be desired when choice, even if limited, was possible. In some ways, however, the U.S. pattern had some unique aspects, in the greater rights given ex-slaves upon their liberation, in its higher subsequent levels of income and more rapid rates of income growth, and in the marked political changes in the initial decades after emancipation. The post-emancipation period in the United States was not one of unidirectional change but rather one of several eras or sequences of time with significantly different patterns of behavior and control.

34. See Green (1976). The role of tariff policy was among the issues discussed in the 1842 and 1848 parliamentary hearings on the West Indian colonies. See also Buxton (1888), 1:59, 96–97, 125. In the 1830s and 1840s, attempts to permit sugar producers to maintain profits used selective tariffs, and these were seen as

For the southern economy as a whole, there was a sharp initial drop in income after 1860 and before 1870 (of almost 40 percent), but after that, per capita income probably grew as rapidly in the South as in the North, during the northern period of substantial industrialization. So sharp was the southern decline, due to the changing labor institutions, however, that it took about a quarter century for the South to recover its antebellum level of income. It appears that the once-for-all decline with the ending of slavery was more important for lowering relative southern income levels than was any period of prolonged stagnation. And those who have emphasized the difficulties of the southern economy in the 1890s and 1930s, as indicating the permanent difficulties of an economy adjusting to having been a slave economy, must consider the implications of southern per capita income growth at a rate at least equal to that of the North from about 1870 to 1950. Moreover, by 1990, the South had almost caught up with the North in terms of per capita income, its income being about 90 percent that of the North.[35] Clearly, there was a substantially long lag in catching up with the North and problems developed related to Jim Crow and other issues, but after the initial decline, the southern economy did not stagnate. The South regained its role as the world's largest cotton producer about a decade after the Civil War and maintained it until about 1920. Cotton was probably a higher share of southern agricultural output after the war than before, and various industrial sectors in the South were also expanding.

a means of helping the colonies to produce sugar and justify emancipation. The planters believed that tariff protection was part of the agreed-upon emancipation agreement, but it did not last long.

35. See Heim (2000), 102. The 1900 ratio was approximately 50 percent.

The impact of emancipation upon southern blacks was somewhat mixed, but in some ways it was quite different before 1890 from what it was to be after. While some argue that concentration on only certain aspects and statistics may lead us to be overly positive in describing the changes that came with emancipation, there are several ways in which the period from 1865 to 1890 provided a more favorable set of conditions for the ex-slaves than did the half century after 1890.[36]

The initial response at the war's end was to free the slaves immediately, with no compensation paid either to slave owners for their losses or to slaves for their prior captivity and forced labor. The loss to the former slave owners was limited by their ability to maintain their lands for productive purposes, as was the case in most other emancipations. The reduction in the labor input by ex-slaves, however, did mean some reduction in land values. The one key exception to former slave owners retaining control of the land was Haiti, since its constitution prevented landownership by whites.[37] The failure to provide "forty acres and a mule" to ex-slaves was regarded as quite a costly broken promise or absent commitment in the South, but given that a hypothetical "eighty acres and two mules" left whites in poverty in the 1890s, it is not clear what the direct long-term economic—in contrast to possible political—benefits of that policy would have been.

36. Boahen (1987), 1, 27–29, points to a similar loss of sovereignty by Africans starting between 1880 and 1900, as well as the losses in Southeast Asia, a period after the ending of the slave trade.

37. See the descriptions of the Haitian constitution of 1805 in Dubois (2004b), 300. It stated that "no white, no matter his nation" could become a "master or property owner." What happened to the free black and mulatto landowners before the 1790s is even more controversial. See Leyburn (1941), 32–42, 238–41.

The U.S. emancipation can be regarded as permitting entry into citizenship by the ex-slaves, and the terms compared favorably in some respects with the rules of citizenship regarding immigrants from Europe.[38] European migrants were required to complete residency requirements before attaining citizenship and the right to vote. In several New England states, literacy requirements were introduced in the 1850s with the aim of reducing the foreign vote; by contrast, ex-slaves were granted voting rights immediately, could hold office at all levels throughout the nation, and did not confront literacy tests until another quarter century had passed. (And, at that time, more northern than southern states maintained literacy tests, generally aimed at European and Asian immigrants.)[39] Several southern states passed black codes to control black labor, but these were relatively soon held to be illegal.[40] States and localities in the South, aided by funds from blacks and northerners, private and governmental, placed money into educating the ex-slave population and their children. There was a sharp rise in black schooling expenditures then, equal to about one-third of the white amount per pupil, and in literacy among blacks, increases that would later slow down but were not reversed.[41]

Within agriculture, the plantation as a producing unit declined sharply, and most ex-slaves became workers on small farms—whether as owners, as renters, or as laborers. Incomes and wealth accumulation grew rapidly from their obviously

38. For some interesting comparisons, see Wang (1997). For some description of immigration, see Engerman (2002a).

39. On voting and its changes over time, see Keyssar (2000), Kousser (1974), Rusk (2001), and Engerman and Sokoloff (2005).

40. See T. Wilson (1965).

41. See Margo (1990). Black literacy rose from 20.1 percent in 1870 to 43.2 in 1890 to 69.5 in 1910. Carter et al. (2006), 2:468, as prepared by Claudia Goldin.

low starting point. There was considerable geographic mobility within the South by the black (and white) population. The share of southern farms owned and operated by blacks rose from virtually nothing in 1860 to reach over 20 percent in 1880 and 1890.[42]

These commercial developments, while still leaving a large gap in relative black and white economic conditions, suggest that there was some reason to maintain positive expectations about what ex-slaves could achieve, at least in the absence of even more direct, terribly oppressive controls and limitations. In politics, blacks could vote and hold office, at all levels, up to the national Senate.[43] Ex-slaves did not vote as a monolithic bloc, as indicated by Thomas Holt for South Carolina, Charles Vincent for Louisiana, and Michael Fitzgerald for Mobile, Alabama. Holt, for example, has pointed out that mulattoes in South Carolina had different patterns of voting on economic policy issues than did blacks. It seems quite doubtful, however, that even bloc voting by blacks and mulattoes would have allowed the ex-slaves to avoid the deterioration in their conditions in subsequent decades.[44]

In the United States, as elsewhere, the reimposition of slavery in its earlier form was not a major issue politically, and there were few attempts to return legally to that previous condition. There were obvious attempts to introduce restrictions that

42. See Oubre (1978), S. Holt (2000), and Penningroth (2003). This was probably a higher share of land ownership by lower classes than in Cuba, Mexico, and Argentina. Prior to the Civil War, there was some free black and slave ownership of property in land and other slaves, but these were too low to account for the postbellum pattern. See Kenzer (1997) and Schweninger (1990) for antebellum-postbellum comparisons. For comparisons of changing literacy by ex-slaves and free blacks, see Sacerdote (2005).

43. From 1865 to 1900, there were twenty-two blacks in Congress (two in the Senate and twenty in the House), of whom thirteen had been former slaves. See Ragsdale and Treese (1990), Foner (1988), and Franklin and Moss (1994).

44. See T. Holt (1977), Vincent (1976), and Fitzgerald (2002).

would have a similar effect, even without the ability to buy and sell people and to have the complete status enforced. This initial, somewhat hopeful set of events was to be reversed in 1890, with the putting into place of policies that were to persist for about a half century. This sharp break in southern race relations was earlier noted by C. Vann Woodward in *The Strange Career of Jim Crow,* a book some criticize for what they believe was its suggestion that racism was not significant in the South before 1890. That criticism, however, was on a point that was not really central to Woodward's argument.[45] Woodward had made the crucial point that what happened in the South after 1890 was quite different from what had occurred before, a claim that, with other works, has led to a major reinterpretation of racism in the United States and elsewhere.[46] A similar change in the southern racial system was later argued for by Howard Rabinowitz, who claimed that the repressive legislation at the end of the nineteenth century was due to the successes, not failures, of blacks after emancipation. That meant that, despite continued segregation, blacks could make some progress in the postbellum urban South, even without real social integration.[47]

The changes in the 1890s were determined by that decade's collapse in the cotton market, influencing all producers, whites as well as blacks. This generated political, economic, and social turmoil and led to a major shift in policies toward blacks in the South. The 1880s had seen legislation and legal interpretation that provided a partial return to some aspects of a plantation

45. Woodward (1974). For an "optimistic" picture of the initial outcome of emancipation, see Higgs (1977).

46. See Cell (1982) for an argument of a changing basis of racism in the postbellum South. See also Fredrickson (2002).

47. Rabinowitz (1978).

system, shifting some of the southern basis of agricultural production to a system with more labor controls even without a return to the full gang system.[48] In the 1890s, there was significant legislation providing literacy tests and grandfather clauses, which sharply reduced black voting in the South, the region where most U.S. blacks still lived before World War I.[49]

It was not until after World War II that blacks were able to regain their earlier voting rights. Without black voting power, the nature of southern education expenditures shifted sharply. In 1890, the expenditure per black pupil was about one-third of that per white pupil; by 1910, the ratio was about one-fifth to one-tenth.[50] It took several decades for this change to be reversed. The 1890s saw various pieces of state legislation, such as the Jim Crow laws, restricting black occupations, residential patterns, and transportation rights. At the national level, the Supreme Court decided *Plessy v. Ferguson* in 1896, a decision affecting transportation, education, and other rights, not reversed for sixty years. The level of violence in the South, always high before, during, and after the Civil War, became more marked, with increases in the number of lynchings and a shift to a considerably higher ratio of blacks to whites lynched.[51]

Violence was not unknown in other post-emancipation societies, but such incidents were more often described as responses to political uprisings and citizens' riots, rather than the controls imposed by lynchings, which were privately, not legislatively, organized by relatively small groups, even if acquiesced in by the police power of the state. A particularly interesting case of mili-

48. This shift has been well described by Woodman (1995).

49. See Kousser (1974).

50. See Margo (1990).

51. See Tolnay and Beck (1995) and Brundage (1993).

tary control in response to what is generally described as a political disturbance occurred in Cuba in the year 1912. While this is often described as a political conflict, not a racial disturbance, almost all of the several thousand killed were Afro-Cubans and several of the eight white deaths were apparently due to friendly fire.[52] The estimated deaths in a period of less than two months were, however, at least as great as the number lynched in the U.S. South between 1880 and 1950. Even if the present estimates of deaths in this disturbance in Cuba are too high, as some now argue, the nature of the Cuban racial response to emancipation bears further analysis. This is suggested by the long persistence of low ratios of black-white literacy rates and black landownership rates in Cuba, relative to those in the United States.[53]

Looking at the significant changes in southern racial attitudes since emancipation poses several interesting questions, as does the study of the racism of the North after its earlier slave emancipation. The initial black response to the ending of slavery suggests that the slave experience did not prevent many individuals and families from dealing with their economic and educational needs. Immediate postwar responses in terms of black production, saving, and investing behavior were reflected in some (limited) success in land acquisition and use. The desire for

52. See Helg (1995), 193–226. Afro-Cubans benefited from the passage of universal male suffrage in 1902 (128). See de la Fuente (2001), 56–95, and Scott (2005), 216–52.

53. See Helg (1995), 129–30, and Schroeder (1982). Not only were black literacy rates lower in Cuba than in the United States in the early decades of the twentieth century, the ratio of black literacy to white literacy was roughly equal. De la Fuente (2001), 106, 142, 310, shows a sharp narrowing of the black-white literacy for those between the ages of ten and nineteen in the twentieth century, a pattern similar to that in the U.S., while the ratio of black high school and college graduates in Cuba (and Brazil) in the 1980s was considerably smaller than

education, for themselves and their families, and the reduction in female labor force participation in agriculture, even at some cost in terms of debt persistence and health, suggest that adaptability to their new conditions was possible and could, given the then-existing levels of white resistance at the time, be accomplished. There were clear indications of work skills and some ability to utilize the market to achieve gains, and this meant dealing with problems similar to those of the whites of comparable income and occupational level. Also, it raises the question of what is meant by the legacy of slavery and how long and under what conditions it endured. What aspects of black behavior and belief in the present day could be considered primarily due to the prior existence of slavery and what reflects more the response to subsequent problems in postbellum society?

V

Several recent important debates pose this question of the meaning of the legacy of slavery. The link of postbellum racism, or rather its specific formulation, to racial attitudes under slavery points to the possible emergence of a different form of racism after emancipation, a point raised also about the timing of the rise of a new racism in the European world.[54] The somewhat related question of whether the racism of the 1890s was independently arrived at by lower classes or whether they were duped into these beliefs by a defensive strategy developed by

---

in the U.S. Landownership by blacks in 1931 Cuba was about one-tenth that of whites. See de la Fuente (2001), 106. Illegitimacy rates for "coloreds" in Cuba, between 1899 and 1931, were over 60 percent, and for whites the ratio was about one-third. Nelson (1950), 199. And in the Cuban Senate and House in 1945, less than 10 percent of the members were colored. Nelson (1950), 157.

54. See Cell (1982) and Drescher (1999).

the upper classes to prevent a black-white coalition still attracts attention.[55] The economic legacy of slavery in the South did not prevent the South from starting to converge on the North in terms of per capita income after 1900, and for the South to basically catch up by the end of the twentieth century. If there is a "New South" or several New Souths, it remains to be seen when they arose and whether they replaced or moderated the legacy of slavery. Was the innovation of air-conditioning as significant a development for the South as was the cotton gin or the organization of rice production?[56]

There is another issue for which it is claimed that the legacy of slavery remains critical and of major importance—the study of the present-day black family in the United States.[57] This debate goes back to the abolitionists, particularly Theodore Weld, as well as to subsequent black scholars, including W. E. B. Du Bois and E. Franklin Frazier. The single-parent household and out-of-wedlock births, both traditionally higher among black families, are even today often attributed to the legacy of slavery, at least by those who believe these are undesirable patterns and feel the need to avoid "blaming the victim." Although the rates have been higher for blacks than for whites in the United States, they remain much lower than those for ex-slaves in Jamaica and elsewhere in the British West Indies.[58]

Not all antislavery advocates have argued that the slave family was relatively unstable, a contention made by some slave

55. For a presentation of this debate, see Williamson (1984).

56. On these innovations, technical and organizational, see Carney (2001), Lakwete (2003), and Cooper (1998).

57. For a recent presentation of this argument, one long familiar in the historical literature, see J. Q. Wilson (2002).

58. See Roberts (1957).

owners and an aspect of the proslavery defense. In writings before the Depression, Frazier had painted a more positive picture
of the slave family than he did later, and he also listed other
causes of black family instability after emancipation, including
the post–Civil War chaos, the migration to the North, and, later,
the Great Depression.[59] Debates among historians such as Eugene Genovese, Herbert Gutman, Larry Hudson, and Brenda
Stevenson have made the picture of the slave family less clear
than we used to believe.[60] What is striking, however, is the nature of the changes over time in black illegitimacy rates and in
the percentages of female-headed households, with these increasing sharply as we get further removed from slavery and as
economic circumstances seemingly improve. The ratios of black
households headed by females have risen from about 20–25 percent for 1870 to 1930, to about 30 percent in the 1960s (when
Moynihan wrote his famous report, which stressed the importance of current economic conditions), to over 50 percent in the
1990s, a long-delayed and clearly accelerating instance of what
some call a legacy. Intervening and current events, both in the
private sector and in government policy, would seem to have an
important impact in addition to any legacy of slavery in explaining the pattern.[61] This question of the legacy of slavery can, of
course, be applied to many other aspects of the black experience,
not just family questions.

59. Frazier (1939).

60. Genovese (1974), Gutman (1976), Hudson (1997), and Stevenson (1996).

61. Engerman (1977), and for post–World War II data, Thernstrom and Thernstrom (1997), 238, 240, and W. J. Wilson (1987), 63–66. The rising trend in illegitimate births is even more dramatic, rising from 22 percent in 1960 to 70 percent
in 1994. While the rates of illegitimate births and of female-headed households
for whites have increased since World War II, their magnitudes remain considerably below those of blacks.

In the debates within the United States, racism is generally related to slavery, as cause as well as consequence. It should be noted, in perspective, that, in the world at large, we have had racism without slavery (both before emancipation and after slavery was no longer deemed acceptable), and we have examples of racism leading to exclusion, segregation, expulsion, and killing rather than slavery. Moreover, slavery has existed without traditional forms of racism (particularly in Africa and Asia), and there has been widespread poverty and mass killing, in war and otherwise, without either racism or slavery. Indeed, the number of killings without slavery or racism, in nationalistic and religious warfare, famines, and civil wars, quite possibly exceeds the number of those who were ever enslaved.

There is another point about emancipation that indicates another dramatic change from the world of the nineteenth century, regarding issues of the direction of compensation for past events. As pointed out, in most cases of slavery and serfdom the state provided compensation or passed legislation to have slaves provide compensation to be paid to slave owners to cover part or all of their loss of property rights. Some discussed payments to the slaves for the economic and psychological costs of enslavement, but such payments generated little support and were never implemented. It was only after the 1870s, and then more recently after the 1960s, that payments for various psychological and financial losses to blacks, including the impact of slavery, were proposed.[62] Such payments, now called reparations, were to be made, generally by the state, to individuals for the past burdens that either they or, more frequently, their ancestors faced. In some cases, reparations were to be made to individuals and

62. See Bittker (1973), Robinson (2000), and Berry (2005).

families who actually suffered, but in the case of slavery they are intended for groups or races that have suffered in the past, since none of those who directly experienced slavery are still alive. The complexity of this issue comes from deciding who should pay, who should receive the money, and how large this payment should be. Should reparations come from descendants of former slave owners, descendants of U.S. residents in 1860, or all, including immigrants, in the country at the present time? We may agree on reparations for U.S. slavery, but what about the costs of West Indian slavery, particularly for those then migrating to the United States, reparations for the costs of segregation, or reparations for the losses to potential immigrants who were legally excluded from the United States and also those remaining behind who suffered lower incomes? Clearly, the idea of reparations to blacks, as a principle, fits in much better with current morality than does the past belief in compensation to former slave owners on the basis of property rights. While the claim for reparations serves as an important rhetorical device in arguing for redistributive policies, difficulties of implementation have probably made it uncertain as a specific policy measure today.

The initial optimistic attitudes toward immediate emancipation were captured by Fredrick Douglass. In 1862 he rejected arguments that slaves "can't take care of themselves" and claimed that, rather than being taken care of, "let us stand upon our own legs, work with our own hands, and eat bread in the sweat of our own brows." In short: "let him *alone;* his right of choice as much deserves respect and protection as your own." He comments that, "when you, our white fellow-countrymen, have attempted to do anything for us, it has generally been to deprive us of some right, power or privilege which you would die before you would submit to have taken from you." While Douglass presented no specifics as to particular policies, the general thrust of his preferred policies is clear. Twenty years later, he pointed to the "mental, moral, and material improvement" of the ex-slaves, particularly in regard to education and property acquisition, even though "no people were ever emancipated under conditions more unfavorable for good results," "without money, land, or friends and, worst of all, under the fierce resentment of those who owned the land from which he must obtain his bread."[63] Although left "free to starve," their population increased more rapidly than did the whites, despite the many predictions that the race would die out. While possibly accepting that an appropriate, more interventionist government and white policy might have been desired in 1865, Douglass's statement of black gains and ultimate progress does reflect the spirit of conditions in the 1870s and 1880s.

63. Douglass (1984), 373–88.

SLAVERY AND ITS CONTINUITIES IN THE MODERN WORLD

AS WE HAVE SEEN, slavery has long existed and had been present in most parts of the world before the era of emancipations. Although nominally free populations have generally exceeded slave populations in most instances, slavery did play an important economic and social role in many different places. In most cases, political, economic, and religious principles advocated humane treatment of the enslaved; manumissions of individuals and families were considered to be praiseworthy actions.[1] Bad treatment by owners could, in some cases, be legally punished. Slaves could resist, run away, or form Maroon communities, but these, while disruptive, were not generally seen as leading to the end of the slave system. Indeed, Maroons often had formal or informal arrangements with white slave owners, though this worked against existing slaves.

Such constraints, however, did not form the basis of a systematic attack on the system of slavery or present an argument that slavery should no longer be permitted to exist. The practice had long existed in human society and, even in the eighteenth century and later, few observers believed that there was any reason to anticipate that slavery would cease at any time in the immediate future.

1. See, e.g., the Siete Partidas and the Koran, among the many possible sources. For a discussion of the relation between slavery and freedom in broad historical perspectives, see Patterson (1991).

The change in attitude toward slavery as a system developed from new sets of philosophical and religious ideas that emerged in western Europe in the seventeenth and eighteenth centuries. One philosophical movement, the Enlightenment, advocated the centrality of individual rights, particularly for those regarded as insiders, and was critical of the domination of one individual insider by another.[2] The belief in the rights of individuals was also to be contrasted with beliefs in those societies that emphasized the importance of community and communal roles, of the value of belonging to a society, and of having a somewhat set position in a fixed hierarchy.[3] And, while Enlightenment thinkers initially did regard some groups as outsiders and therefore subject to some limitations on their rights, ultimately the Enlightenment did expand its definitions to include all of humankind as nonenslaveable, even if still subject to major differences in other rights. Also important in the attack on slavery as a system was the extension of religious ideas, particularly those related to Protestantism, concerning the rights of individuals and the ability to deal directly with the deity.[4]

The Enlightenment did have some mixed effects over time in its impact on human rights. At the same time that it began

2. From the rather extensive writing on the Enlightenment I have found particularly useful D. Williams (1999), for its collection of readings, and Outram (2005), for its analysis.

3. The long debate on communalism versus individualism remains an important issue, both for historical examination and for current cultural politics. Clearly, community feeling and belongingness have some attraction today, but they may also come with some form of hierarchy, which has advantages for some but incurs costs to others. Belief in caste, "natural slavery," and "networks of protective power" have been used to defend the social system of slavery. See Patterson (1982), 27–28, on the importance of communal protection in some societies.

4. See D. B. Davis (1984), which also presents a more jaundiced view of the

to deal with individualism and freedom for whites, western Europeans began, or continued, to justify slavery of Africans in Europe and in the Americas, as well as the coercion of Indians in the Americas. Also, after the middle of the fifteenth century, ending slavery was held to be consistent with the expansion of serfdom for whites within Europe. Among Europeans, however, slavery was now restricted to those of a different race. Those who were enserfed in Europe, while of the same race, were often held to be different because of their presumed limited intellectual and/or moral capabilities. These limitations also were argued to be characteristics of peasants in many societies, justifying legal constraints on behavior, even for those legally free.[5] In many societies, even today, a belief in limited mental and moral capacities underlies the argument for the need for control and coercion of otherwise legally free persons, including their laboring, and for restrictions on their right to vote.

II

After some attempts at enslavement of Native Americans—fraught with problems of economic feasibility, given the difficulties of enslavement near the location where the enslaved lived, as well as debates as to its morality—the early arguments of the Spanish jurist Las Casas ultimately meant that New World slavery was restricted to black Africans.[6] Whites could be sent as indentured labor and as convicts to work in the Americas and could be serfs in Europe, while Native Americans could be sub-

---

impact of the Enlightenment. For a positive presentation of the antislavery role of the Catholic Church, see Stark (2003), 329–37, 343–44.

5. See Blum (1978), Hellie (1982), and Freedman (1999).

6. The issue of enslaving individuals distant from their place of residence was also important in explaining the pattern of slavery in Africa.

ject to various types of labor coercion in Latin America, some resembling the controls used prior to the arrival of the Spanish, since Native Americans enslaved other Native Americans prior to European arrival. Yet only enslavement of blacks transported from Africa was regarded as acceptable in the settlement of the Americas. Indian slaves, even when legally enslaved, were generally small in numbers and replaced over time with blacks.

Nevertheless, by the start of the nineteenth century, these same Europeans in western Europe and North and South America were the only groups anywhere in the world responsible for a major, concerted attack on the system of slavery. Their critique of slavery was not really original in its economic and psychological aspects, since many of their arguments went back to the classical world. Rather, the debate focused on the question of who can be regarded as human and, thus, automatically qualify to be free of slavery. The Enlightenment ideals have thus been considered as providing both a basis for African slavery as well as for its disappearance.

III

The disagreement about the relative importance of moral versus economic factors in ending New World slavery remains a major debate today. The economic argument has included several possible dimensions—the unprofitability of slavery, the declining importance of slavery in the economy, or the political disputes among several economic groups. To the nineteenth-century British historian William Lecky's claim that "the unwearied, unostentatious, and inglorious crusade of England against slavery may probably be regarded as among the three or four perfectly virtuous acts recorded in the history of nations," Eric Williams countered that "the decisive forces in the period of history we have discussed are the developing economic forces," and "the political and moral ideas of the age are to be examined in the very closest relation to the economic development."[7] This view of the role of economic forces has also been used to minimize the importance of moral and political factors in abolition in both European and non-European areas with slavery.[8]

With free labor, even with some significant economic constraints, which persisted with the ending of slavery and serfdom, there were numerous dramatic changes in ways of living and working. There were changes in the nature of labor control and working conditions, in patterns of population mobility, and, ultimately, in political rights, with the definition of freedom ultimately resting upon legal disputes to establish the permissible amount of control.

Workers now had, legally, choices as to type of work and occupations they sought and were also able to make their own choices of location regarding places of work and of residence. They could select the size of units in which they wished to work, seek to influence their wages by individual and collective action, and exercise some choices regarding the intensity of work. Such freedoms were, of course, not complete, since the need to subsist and to provide for a family meant that individuals did confront

7. See Lecky (1869), 1:161, and E. Williams (1944), 209–12. Williams claims that we can understand the confusions in the interpretations of the ending the slave trade at the time, because of what the contemporaries wish to present, but that "historians, writing a hundred years after, have no excuse for continuing to wrap the real interests in confusion." Writing about British historians and the West Indies some two decades later, Williams (1966), 233, states that "the British historians wrote almost as if Britain had introduced Negro slavery solely for the satisfaction of abolishing it."

8. See Drescher (1999) for a recent set of evaluations of abolition movements. The economic argument is complex, since for any action taken, there are some who benefit and some who lose, so there are always some economic benefits to be pointed to, and the balance of political power is critical.

some limited freedoms of action because of low incomes and the necessity for laboring. Also, contractual arrangements covering only a specific and limited period of work could lead to dissatisfaction with the terms of labor during the contract period and thus be regarded as a form of slavery, not freedom, even if the initial contract were believed voluntary. Thus, for example, Cicero claimed that any individual who labored for another was, for that period, to be regarded as a slave, a point earlier made in Assyrian law and one that can lead to significant disagreement about the status of labor even today.[9]

Without a means of redesigning the system of income distribution, wealth distribution, and political power, certain imbalances in political and economic power among individuals in society will persist even with emancipation and legal freedom. The questions of whether the constraints arise from the lack of sufficient income to avoid poverty, thus limiting the usefulness of the choice to be exercised, and whether the legal limits imposed by the political system on mobility, economic or geographic, are to be regarded as leading to unfree labor and a return to slavery remain debated. Even without the ability to buy and sell people there are clearly important limits on free populations, and it is these limits that are often considered to make contemporary conditions equivalent to slavery in the past.

Low standards of living have existed for slave and free workers, but the legal conditions were often dramatically different, and of course the opportunities for economic and political betterment became greater with the ending of slavery, even if these benefits were to be achieved by the ex-slaves only slowly and over a long period. As some argue, it might be difficult to

9. See Cicero (1913), 153, and Weber (1976), 95–97. See also Tomlins (1985) and Steinfeld (2001).

consider the very impoverished to be as free as are those with higher incomes, and it has been claimed that there should be more sympathetic legal treatment for those in need than for others, as "necessity sets property aside," and "extreme want of food or clothing justified theft."[10]

This depiction of free labor as being in binary opposition to slave labor conveys the spirit of the nineteenth-century antislavery argument, obviously to the great advantages of free labor as a system. The clear-cut distinction, however, has been modified by descriptions of freedom as a spectrum of characteristics, including limitations on what some regard as crucial aspects of freedom, and which can impose slavelike constraints by economic, political, or police power. The Marxian skepticism about what free labor actually meant is conveyed by the term "wage slavery," while the use of criminal sanctions to enforce labor contracts as part of Master and Servant Acts is not easily reconcilable with some common notions of free labor. The set of controls over ex-slaves in the British colonial empire and in the United States were seen as one form of slavery replacing another, and the many forms of bonded and contract slavery today, including child labor, sex trafficking, sweatshops, and debt bondage, as well as Nazi camps and the Soviet Gulag, are examples of cases to which some wish to apply the term "slavery," whether for rhetorical or other purposes.[11]

10. Novak (1996), 72, quoting Thomas Rutherford (1799). See also Grotius (1925), 148–50, 193–95, and Pufendorf (1991), 53–55, for earlier statements of the argument, described by Pufendorf as "necessity knows no laws." Hont (2005), 94–95, 413–26, discusses these arguments, along with similar points raised by Hume and by Smith.

11. See Bales (1999) and Miers (2003), whose definitions suggest that the numbers in slavery are at an all-time high, certainly absolutely but possibly also as a percentage of the population.

To cover all the dimensions of freedom and free labor is a complex task, and any attempted index seeking a unique ranking will undoubtedly contain some inconsistencies. Thus a simple measure of freedom for purposes of comparison is of rather doubtful value. In most cases, slave emancipation did not provide political suffrage to those freed, but at the time of slave emancipation neither were voting rights available to many members of the free populations in these societies, with the major exceptions of Canada and the United States. Women generally were not given the vote until the twentieth century, while for adult males the right to vote was often based on requirements regarding literacy or financial considerations: tax payments or property values. Another group of potential new citizens (besides the ex-slaves) of the United States after 1865, immigrants from Europe, faced residency and citizenship requirements at the local, state, and national levels before being allowed to vote. And those arriving in the United States later in the nineteenth century from China and Japan found that they would not be able to vote for some decades.[12] Within Europe, suffrage expansion was long delayed after the ending of serfdom, and in some nations of the Americas there was a very substantial lag after the ending of slavery before suffrage was widely granted.[13] Even within societies where some members had some significant rights, they were often lacking in others, and not all members of societies had the same set of basic rights.

Free labor societies were, moreover, seldom free of the effects of insider-outsider distinctions, and these often served to provide constraints on individual and group behavior. At times, these limits were imposed by positive governmental actions; at

12. See Keyssar (2000), Rusk (2001), and Engerman and Sokoloff (2005).
13. See the tables in Engerman and Sokoloff (2005).

others they were privately organized and implemented, but with government acquiescence. Such individual and group differences have been based on ethnicity, nationality, and race and have led to differences in behavior toward, and treatment of, others, leading to differences in incomes, occupations, and voting rights. Free labor within a nation, for which foreign immigration and/ or emigration is prohibited, is not the same as worldwide free labor, and the international flow of labor has remained a major source of conflict even in a world without slavery.

After the nineteenth century, many nations introduced restrictions on immigration. Even when in-migration was permitted, there were delays before the full rights of citizenship and suffrage were granted. Whereas restrictions on immigration were widespread by the twentieth century, in earlier periods, at least as important were those restrictions in Europe and Asia imposed on emigration, so that people could not leave their home nations with earned capital, or else before they had fulfilled military or educational obligations.[14] A belief in the importance of nationality has long permitted some limits on freedom of population movement, both outward and inward, in addition to the effects of national origin on the movement of goods and capital, via tariff barriers and controls over capital flows. Such restrictions can impose costs on the residents of both donor and host nations and have a major impact on living standards, whatever the legal status of the population.

Ethnicity has long been a cause of restrictions imposed on the behavior of individuals within societies, often influencing occupational choice and the ability to select locations for residence. Similarly, age and gender have limited free choice, as do laws regarding vagrancy, poor law provisions (with their impact

14. Engerman (2002a).

on locational decisions and mobility), and provisions for relief and unemployment insurance. Allowances for the basic provision of safety nets, useful for preventing starvation or malnutrition, have had an influence on the ability of people to choose. And systems of labor law, such as the British Master and Servant Acts (with their threats of jailing for leaving work), while not leading to what all might describe as slavery, did provide limits on what legally free persons could do, even in the late nineteenth century, many years after the time ended in which these people could legally be bought and sold.[15]

The British master and servant codes, dating from 1562 and lasting until 1875, spread throughout the British colonial empire from the times of settlement into the twentieth century. While differences in terms and constraints did develop between areas, the basic provisions were generally quite similar. The aim of this legislation was to get people to work, to keep them from departing particular jobs by legal enforcement of long-term contracts, and also, at times, to set wage rates at below-market standards. The main aspects of non-freedom here were forcing entry into the labor force and creating difficulties in leaving employment when there was a long-term contract. These limitations do not, however, mean that people were unable initially to choose their places of employment and residence. In some periods, however, the British Poor Laws did interfere with migration decisions. Even when there is some element of free choice in accepting employment and agreeing to contracts, the constraining provisions are argued to resemble some aspects of slavery, in preventing people from achieving what they desire. This is so particularly when choices are based on misleading information and lead to undesirable living and working conditions.

15. See Steinfeld (2001) and Hay and Craven (2004).

IV

The economic argument for the superior performance of free, rather than slave, labor had come to play a major part in the eighteenth- and nineteenth-century debate on slavery. The antislavery argument made the claim that free labor was either less costly (because of higher productivity due to its incentive effects, but not, it was claimed, due to lower costs via less consumption by free workers) or more efficient than was slave labor. A change from slave to free labor, thus, would benefit, via higher output, all members of society, including possibly also the slave owners. The most familiar of these arguments was made by Adam Smith in his claim that, since slaves lacked incentives and an ability to choose employment, they would be unproductive and not innovative.[16] This contention, widely adopted in the antislavery literature because of Smith's reputation, would have been a surprise to many slave owners and to the ancient Greeks, who had also discussed this problem. Xenophon, who had apparently been an estate manager, worked out a system to provide incentives to slave labor even when they were paid in kind—actual goods—not cash. He merely purchased different qualities of clothing and rewarded better workers with better clothes.[17]

Smith's incentive argument, moreover, was somewhat inconsistent with his own description of the different effects on the slaves of French and British owners in the Caribbean, since he argues for better management leading to the superior effectiveness of French slave labor and cheaper sugar from the French

16. See Smith (1976), 2:683–86. Aspects of the incentive argument regarding slave labor have been applied to the case of free labor. Early arguments for piece wages pointed to their advantage relative to the lack of incentives provided by time wages. See Anderson (1789), 7–9. For arguments to introduce slavery to the British prior to the first half of the eighteenth century, see Rozbicki (2001).

17. Xenophon (1990), 336.

islands.[18] The task system, utilized primarily in rice production in South Carolina and elsewhere, was another way to provide incentives and to permit some dispersion in the distribution of income among slaves.[19] A related, but ultimately unsuccessful, attempt at an incentive scheme for indentured labor was the linking of the length of contract to the number of tasks performed rather than, as was almost always done, to the length of time worked.[20]

But the claim of the great inherent economic efficiency of free labor was not the only argument presented for the presumed benefits to society from free labor. Smith's friend David Hume, among others, thought that slaves were too well kept and did not confront the poverty and hunger that were such important incentives for free labor. The value of hunger in getting more labor input was frequently claimed.[21] Another contemporary of Smith, James Steuart, pointed to the different economic aspects of slave and free labor in describing the transition from slave to free societies. In the past, Steuart argued, people worked "because they were slaves to others"; now people work "because they are slaves to their own wants."[22] To raise output in a free labor society requires what some might regard as self-

18. Smith (1976), 2:585–90.

19. For a survey of this issue, see Morgan (1982).

20. This was discussed in Trinidad and British Guiana, but it was apparently neither successful nor widely used. See Laurence (1994), 133–34, 149.

21. Hume (1987), 128, 266–67, acknowledges his "odd position, that the poverty of the common people in France, Italy, and Spain, is, in some measure, owing to the superior riches of the soil and happiness of the climate." More generally, "no people living between the tropics, could ever yet attain to any art or civility . . . while few nations in the temperate climates have been altogether deprived of these advantages." The explanation is that in warmer climates there is less necessity to labor and acquire goods.

22. Steuart (1966), 1:43–55.

coercion, whether based on individual belief, false consciousness, or imposed hegemony from other groups, any of which could set high individual standards for desired consumption. This desire for goods (as opposed to leisure) influenced the willingness to work, the nature of work, the number of hours worked, and the intensity of labor. Of the two arguments, the one with greater appeal to the abolitionists was clearly that stressing the role of greater incentives in leading to higher productivity. This argument for higher free labor productivity, proslavery advocates claimed, however, was empirically not correct, as they believed was demonstrated by the U.S. South and various other slave societies both before and after emancipation. The proslavery advocates paid great attention to the events in Haiti and the British West Indies in describing the economic case for the maintenance of slavery.

There were dramatic differences in the nineteenth-century European and American societies in total and per capita income according to whether they were based primarily on free labor or they either maintained slavery or had recently ended slavery. The perceived differences in growth of income were used to justify a belief in the superiority of free labor.[23] Those Western nations with primarily free labor experienced, by historical standards, rapid rates of economic growth, greatly increasing their incomes relative to those of the rest of the world, whether slave or not.[24]

23. See Temperley (1977) and D. B. Davis (1966, 1975, 1984). For serfdom, see Blum (1978).

24. See the data presented in the table in Maddison (2001), 126, which indicates the dramatic shifts in measured per capita incomes in different parts of the world after 1500. The ratio of per capita income in Asia to that of western Europe falls from about three-quarters in 1500 to about one-quarter in 1870; and for Latin America it is from slightly above one-half in 1500 to above one-third in 1870, and in Africa from about one-half to above one-fifth.

Economic growth was accompanied by major changes in the structure of the economy. Those economies growing rapidly were the first nations to experience the shift of output and of the labor force out of agriculture and into industry and services that has been a standard part of economic modernization. Other aspects of the change to a modern economy included a movement of the population into urban areas, the expansion of the size of producing units in industry based upon a more extensive capital stock, and the systematic development of new techniques and organizations of production based on scientific and technological changes. By referring to these changes as modernization, Marxists and other economists have categorized slave-based agriculture, as well as non-slave-based agriculture, as a relic of the past, lacking the industry presumably needed for economic growth.

Over time, in non-slave or post-slave societies, political systems tended to become more open, with the franchise slowly, sometimes very slowly, being extended to include larger shares of the population (often, however, not until after the start of the twentieth century). This slow expansion characterized societies that did not have slavery as well as those that did, although a specific test for the influence of having had slavery is made difficult, since many formerly slave societies remained parts of colonial empires into the twentieth century. More opportunities for education became available, and literacy became more widespread, often including women as well as men. Some European nations continued their imperialistic ventures into the less developed parts of the world, maintaining political power in these areas even without the imposition of slavery; indeed, the rationale, in some cases, of this expansion was the abolition of slavery. There were negative aspects to this, but these European nations often were the primary force in originating movements to end slavery in Africa and Asia, often against the aims of the local elite in those areas, as well as providing for education and other social services. There was a rather limited antislavery movement outside of the European societies, and Europeans were often the only important, not always successful, antislavery movement at the time, a pattern that may help to explain the often slow decline of slavery worldwide.

v

The relationship between these economic and political changes and the emergence of a successful antislavery movement remains a source of contention among scholars. Whether the antislavery movement developed out of these political, economic, or cultural changes due to changing levels of income has been debated, as has the question of whether the major influence in the abolition movement came from the elite or the laboring classes. And, if economic changes were important, was this due to absolute changes in the productive capabilities of the slave systems, or were they mainly the response to relative differences in incomes between Europe and elsewhere, which emerged based on the characteristics of modernization?[25] While some argue that it was economic decline that led to a widespread consensus to end the slave trade, others point to economic disagreement among various groups in the political elite. The comparison of a long existing slave-based agricultural economy with a newly emerging "modern" industrial society no doubt did much to generate the impression of the relative backwardness of slavery that underlies both the earlier antislavery movement as well as some of the recent interpretations of the antislavery debate.

25. See D. B. Davis (1975, 1984) and Drescher (1987, 2002).

It should not be unexpected that the first major attack on the slave system emerged out of the European Enlightenment and religious beliefs in individual rights and political and economic freedom.[26] Slavery and serfdom were no longer regarded as consistent with these new ideals, particularly, at first, for insiders and then, later, even for those previously considered outsiders. The major focus of antislavery arguments was slavery's impact on the personality of the slaves and their loss of the ability to control their own lives. Dramatic in its effects, the antislavery movement was not, by our modern standards, particularly radical in the sense of generating other major changes in political and economic power. Abolition rarely disturbed existing political structures. In few cases were there initial losses in the political power of the elites, and generally compensation was provided to slave owners, not to slaves. Land was maintained by the former slave owners, and as part of the process of gradual emancipation, the generally existing property rights structure was maintained. The ending, worldwide, of slavery and serfdom took place several centuries after the start of the Enlightenment, and its accomplishments were often incomplete, leaving other aspects of freedom still to be achieved. In its immediate aftermath, emancipation did not necessarily guarantee a population with higher incomes or one with full political rights and freedoms. Nevertheless, over the century or so since emancipation, U.S. blacks and ex-slaves elsewhere have made major relative and absolute progress in income, life expectation and health, education and literacy, and, since the 1960s, political influence—gains of a magnitude that, presumably, would have been impossible if slavery had remained in place.[27] Some changes required government or

26. See D. B. Davis (1966).

27. See the relevant data in the annual issues of the Statistical Abstract of

legal changes; others were the outcome of changing economic forces; still others apparently reflected changes in widely held social beliefs. For example, the number of lynchings decreased in the twentieth century, declining sharply after the 1920s under pressure from the NAACP and other organizations. Although unsuccessful because of southern filibusters, antilynching legislation was introduced in Congress several times after an initial attempt in 1918. In the 1930s, President Roosevelt did speak out against lynching and supported a vote on a federal antilynching bill that had been placed before Congress. An overall decline in the number of lynchings did occur, however, even in the absence of direct federal legislation to end this form of violence legally. Antilynching legislation did not effectively occur until the Civil Rights Act of 1968.[28]

VI

There were some extensions of the issues raised relating to the labor aspects of antislavery accomplishments. These had, initially, a greater impact on European societies and their offshoots than on other parts of the world. These reforms reflected aspects of

---

the United States and in Carter et al. (2006). The gains vary over time and seem influenced by the overall conditions of the economy. See Thernstrom and Thernstrom (1997). Black incomes converge more rapidly on white when there is general economic prosperity, while the periods of relative decline of income and social standards are generally during sluggish growth or overall declines in income. More recently the share of blacks in poverty has fallen from 55.1 percent in 1959 to 23.6 percent in 1999, while the years difference between black and white life expectation fell from 16.5 in 1850 to 5.7 years in 2000. The difference in the rate of infant mortality fell from 123.2 per 1,000 in 1850 to 8.8 per 1,000 in 2000; see Carter et al. (2006), 1:391, 2:431–32, 675. School enrollment rates (ages five to twenty), which differed by 22.5 percentage points in 1900, are now roughly equal.

28. For discussion, see Tolnay and Beck (1995) and Brundage (1993).

the antislavery movement that have emerged out of discussions of appropriate working and living conditions. Starting in the early nineteenth century, there was legislation to enforce labor standards in some European and American economies, particularly in their expanding industrial sectors. These were not immediately very inclusive, the first beneficiaries being women and children, with few laws covering adult men before the twentieth century. Eventually, standards regarding ages of work, hours, and working conditions were also being introduced for the labor force elsewhere in the world, although sometimes not desired by laborers.[29] Only certain economic sectors were covered, with agriculture usually excluded. It was still later that a concern with labor exploitation and setting minimum wage rates and collective labor action emerged. Legislation on slave working conditions, including the various amelioration codes, often preceded the introduction of these labor standards for free workers. Regulations of the slave trade and of slavery preceded constraints concerning the use of free labor and the conditions of transport of free migration.

Also in the nineteenth century, there was a marked expansion in the relief of the unemployed and destitute and a broader safety net than had been provided in earlier times.[30] Although assistance was still reserved only for the "deserving poor," most nations loosened definitions of those in that category and provided more funds for purposes of poverty relief. In some ways, however, the basic structure of relief and welfare has not changed over many centuries. Aid was to be provided the "deserving poor," while others should not be provided funds and should be coerced into working. The definition of "deserv-

29. Engerman (2003).

30. For a broad analysis, see Lindert (2004).

ing poor" has, of course, varied over time, leading to differences in the numbers and types of recipients of aid. The expansion of public and private supports for relief also had a marked impact on the existence of forms of voluntary slavery. Blackstone claimed, for England, that the availability of governmental, church, and privately provided relief ("from the more opulent part of the community") made voluntary slavery unnecessary.[31] And free labor, unlike slave labor, was able to form unions for collective bargaining to bring about improvements in working conditions and wages. Thus, with the ending of slavery, there were introduced, legally, many improvements in the conditions of free workers. Ending slavery and establishing legally free labor was not a social stopping point but rather led to a continuation of benefits for free labor. Nevertheless, at the same time, the nature of laws and their enforcement imposed limits on the extent to which free labor would be regarded as fully free.

VII

As already noted, the legal ending of slavery has not ended the list of evils considered to be slavery or the rhetorical use of the concept of slavery to define a unique system of evil. Many contemporary evils, having nothing to do with the permanent purchase and sale of individuals for lifetime labor and with inherited status, have been described as forms of slavery in order to be argued as major moral evils. Perhaps the analogy is somewhat unnecessary, since we can always regard things as evil even if they are not to be considered as variants of slavery, and such evils seem to exist under just about all political and economic systems. But as the past antislavery movement had benefited from its use of rhetorical devices to bring about great changes,

31. Blackstone (1979), 1:127.

perhaps it is the wish of current users of the term that they too can use this rhetoric, ultimately, as a route to success, similar to that of the earlier movement.[32] After all, the antislavery success is an example that some good things have been achieved in the past and, hopefully, can be realized in the future.

Finally, it is interesting to turn again to Fredrick Douglass and to describe his dissatisfaction with "wage slavery" and related metaphors. In response to the argument that the deaths in the Irish famine demonstrated a greater evil than did slavery, Douglass commented: "The Irishman is poor, but he is *not* a slave. He *may* be in rags, but he is *not* a slave. He is still the master of his own body, and can say with the poet, 'the hand of Douglass is his own.'" He added, "The world is still before him, where to choose, and poor as may be my opinion of the British Parliament, I cannot believe it will sink to such a depth of infamy as to pass a law for the capture of Fugitive Irishmen!" The Irish, according to Douglass, had many rights beyond those of slaves, including the rights to emigrate, to write, to speak, and to "co-operate for the attainment of his rights and the redress of his wrongs."[33] Douglass recognized the oppression and difficulties of the Irish, but, as a possible caveat today, his comments do point out that the use of slavery as a metaphor may sometimes have unexpected effects for understanding the historical and contemporary record, even while it is clearly crucial for seeking current-day reforms.

32. Kevin Bales's (1999) depiction of "Disposable People" (15, 23) as being a new slavery includes many cases of only a temporary duration, the outcome of debt bondage in agriculture (these being approximately ninety times the estimated number of prostitutes). Yet the sense of evil and compulsion has made his analogy a very sympathetic one.

33. Douglass (1982), 258. See also Roediger (1999) and D. B. Davis (1975).

BIBLIOGRAPHY

Allen, Richard B. 1999. *Slaves, Freedmen, and Indentured Laborers in Colonial Mauritius.* Cambridge: Cambridge University Press.

Allison, Robert J. 1995. *The Crescent Obscured: The United States and the Muslim World, 1776–1815.* New York: Oxford University Press.

Anderson, James. 1789. *Observations on Slavery, Particularly with a View to Its Effects on the British Colonies, in the West Indies.* Manchester: J. Harrop.

Aristotle. 1935. *Oeconomica.* Cambridge, MA: Harvard University Press.

———. 1962. *Politics.* Baltimore: Penguin Books.

Austen, Ralph. 1979. "The Trans-Saharan Slave Trade: A Tentative Census." In Henry A. Gemery and Jan S. Hogendorn (eds.), *The Uncommon Market: Essays in the Economic History of the Atlantic Slave Trade.* New York: Academic Press, 23–76.

Bales, Kevin. 1999. *Disposable People: New Slavery in the Global Economy.* Berkeley: University of California Press.

Beckles, Hilary McD. 1990. *A History of Barbados: From Amerindian Settlement to Nation State.* Cambridge: Cambridge University Press.

Bergad, Laird W. 1999. *Slavery and the Demographic and Economic History of Minas Gerais, Brazil, 1720–1888.* Cambridge: Cambridge University Press.

———. 2004. "American Slave Markets during the 1850's: Slave Price Rises in the United States, Cuba, and Brazil in Comparative Perspective." In David Eltis, Frank D. Lewis, and Kenneth L. Sokoloff (eds.), *Slavery in the Development of the Americas.* Cambridge: Cambridge University Press, 219–35.

Bergad, Laird W., García, Fe Iglesias, and Barcia, María del Carman. 1995. *The Cuban Slave Market, 1790–1880*. Cambridge: Cambridge University Press.

Berlin, Ira. 1998. *Many Thousands Gone: The First Two Centuries of Slavery in North America*. Cambridge, MA: Belknap Press.

Berry, Mary Frances. 2005. *My Face Is Black Is True: Callie House and the Struggle for Ex-slave Reparations*. New York: Alfred A. Knopf.

Bittker, Boris I. 1973. *The Case for Black Reparations*. New York: Random House.

Blackstone, William. 1979. *Commentaries on the Laws of England* (4 vols.; first published 1765–1769). Chicago: University of Chicago Press.

Blum, Jerome. 1978. *The End of the Old Order in Rural Europe*. Princeton: Princeton University Press.

Boahen, A. Adu. 1987. *African Perspectives on Colonialism*. Baltimore: Johns Hopkins University Press.

Bodin, Jean. 1962. *The Six Bookes of a Commonweale* (first published 1606). Cambridge, MA: Harvard University Press.

Breeden, James O. (ed.). 1980. *Advice among Masters: The Ideal in Slave Management in the Old South*. Westport: Greenwood Press.

Brooks, James F. 2002. *Captives and Cousins: Slavery, Kinship, and Community in the Southwest Borderlands*. Chapel Hill: University of North Carolina Press.

Brundage, W. Fitzhugh. 1993. *Lynching in the New South: Georgia and Virginia, 1880–1930*. Urbana: University of Illinois Press.

Burns, Robert I., S.J. (ed.). 2001. *Las Siete Partidas* (5 vols.). Philadelphia: University of Pennsylvania Press.

Bushnell, Horace. 1860. *The Census and Slavery (a Thanksgiving discourse, Delivered in the Chapel at Clifton Springs, N.Y., November 29, 1860)*. Hartford: L. E. Hunt.

Buxton, Sydney. 1888. *Finance and Politics: An Historical Study, 1783–1885*. (2 vols.). London: John Murray.

Cairnes, J. E. 1969. *The Slave Power: Its Character, Career and Probable Designs, Being an Attempt to Explain the Real Issues involved in the American Contest* (first published 1862). New York: Harper & Row.

Campbell, Alan B. 1979. *The Lanarkshire Miners: A Social History of Their Trade Unions, 1775–1974.* Edinburgh: John Donald.

Campbell, Gwyn. 2003. "Introduction: Slavery and Other Forms of Unfree Labour in the Indian 'Ocean World.'" *Slavery and Abolition* 24 (August), ix–xxxii.

Carney, Judith A. 2001. *Black Rice: The African Origins of Rice Cultivation in the Americas.* Cambridge, MA: Harvard University Press.

Carter, Susan B., et al. (eds.). 2006. *Historical Statistics of the United States: Earliest Times to the Present.* Millennial Edition (5 vols.). Cambridge: Cambridge University Press.

Cell, John W. 1982. *The Highest Stage of White Supremacy: The Origins of Segregation in South Africa and the American South.* Cambridge: Cambridge University Press.

Cicero. 1913. *De Officiis.* Cambridge, MA: Harvard University Press.

Clarence-Smith, William Gervase, and Topik, Steven (eds.). 2003. *The Global Coffee Economy in Africa, Asia, and Latin America, 1500–1989.* Cambridge: Cambridge University Press.

Clendinnen, Inga. 1991. *Aztecs: An Interpretation.* Cambridge: Cambridge University Press.

Clodfelter, Michael. 1992. *Warfare and Armed Conflicts: A Statistical Reference to Casualty and Other Figures, 1618–1991* (2 vols.). Jefferson: McFarland.

Cobbett, W. 1816. *The Parliamentary History of England from the Earliest Period to the Year 1803.* Vol. 28. *Comprising the Period from the Eighth of May 1789 to the Fifteenth of March 1791.* London: T. C. Hansard.

———. 1817. *The Parliamentary History of England from the Earliest Period to the Year 1803.* Vol. 29. *Comprising the Period from Twenty-second of March 1791 to the Thirteenth of December 1792.* London: T. C. Hansard.

Condorcet, Marquis de. 1999. "Reflections on Black Slavery" (1781). In David Williams (ed.), *The Enlightenment*. Cambridge: Cambridge University Press, 308–16.

Conrad, Robert Edgar. 1972. *The Destruction of Brazilian Slavery, 1850–1888*. Berkeley: University of California Press.

Cooper, Gail. 1998. *Air-Conditioning America: Engineers and the Controlled Environment, 1900–1960*. Baltimore: Johns Hopkins University Press.

Corbitt, Duvon Clough. 1971. *A Study of the Chinese in Cuba, 1847–1947*. Wilmore: Asbury College.

Corris, Peter. 1973. *Passage, Port and Plantation: A History of Solomon Islands Labour Migration, 1870–1914*. Melbourne: Melbourne University Press.

Craton, Michael. 1978. *Searching for the Invisible Man: Slaves and Plantation Life in Jamaica*. Cambridge, MA: Harvard University Press.

Cugoano, Quobna Ottobah. 1999. *Thoughts and Sentiments on the Evil of Slavery and Other Writings* (first published 1787). Harmondsworth: Penguin Books.

Davis, David Brion. 1966. *The Problem of Slavery in Western Culture*. Ithaca: Cornell University Press.

———. 1975. *The Problem of Slavery in the Age of Revolution, 1770–1823*. Ithaca: Cornell University Press.

———. 1984. *Slavery and Human Progress*. Oxford: Oxford University Press.

———. 2006. *Inhuman Bondage: The Rise and Fall of Slavery in the New World*. New York: Oxford University Press.

Davis, Robert C. 2003. *Christian Slaves, Muslim Masters: White Slavery in the Mediterranean, the Barbary Coast, and Italy, 1500–1800*. Houndmills: Palgrave Macmillan.

Deerr, Noel. 1949–1950. *The History of Sugar* (2 vols.). London: Chapman & Hall.

de Groot, Silvia W. 2003. *Surinam Maroon Chiefs in Africa in Search of Their Country of Origin*. Amsterdam: by the author.

de la Fuente, Alejandro. 2001. *A Nation for All: Race, Inequality, and Politics in Twentieth-Century Cuba.* Chapel Hill: University of North Carolina Press.

De Mello, Pedro C. 1992. "Expectation of Abolition and Sanguinity of Coffee Planters in Brazil, 1871–1888." In Robert William Fogel and Stanley L. Engerman (eds.), *Without Consent or Contract: The Rise and Fall of American Slavery.* Technical Papers, vol. 2: *Conditions of Slave Life and the Transition to Freedom.* New York: W. W. Norton, 629–46.

Denevan, William M. (ed.). 1976. *The Native Population of the Americas in 1492.* Madison: University of Wisconsin Press.

Docker, Edward Wybergh. 1970. *The Blackbirders: The Recruiting of South Seas Labour for Queensland, 1863–1907.* Sydney: Angus & Robertson.

Domar, Evsey D. 1970. "The Causes of Slavery or Serfdom: A Hypothesis." *Journal of Economic History* 30 (March), 18–32.

———. 1989. "Were Russian Serfs Overcharged for Their Land by the 1861Emancipation? The History of One Historical Table." In George Grantham and Carol Leonard (eds.), *Agrarian Organization in the Century of Industrialization: Europe, Russia and North America.* Part B. Greenwich: JAI Press, 429–39.

Donald, Leland. 1997. *Aboriginal Slavery on the Northwest Coast of North America.* Berkeley: University of California Press.

Douglass, Frederick. 1969. *My Bondage and My Freedom* (first published 1855). New York: Dover.

———. 1982. *The Frederick Douglass Papers: Series One: Speeches, Debates, and Interviews.* Vol. 2, 1847–54. New Haven: Yale University Press.

———. 1984. *The Narrative and Selected Writings.* New York: Modern Library.

Drescher, Seymour. 1987. *Capitalism and Antislavery: British Mobilization in Comparative Perspective.* New York: Oxford University Press.

———. 1996. "The Atlantic Slave Trade and the Holocaust: A Comparative Analysis." In Alan S. Rosenbaum (ed.), *Is the Holocaust Unique? Perspectives on Comparative Genocide.* Boulder: Westview Press, 65–85.

———. 1999. *From Slavery to Freedom: Comparative Studies in the Rise and Fall of Atlantic Slavery.* New York: New York University Press.

———. 2002. *The Mighty Experiment: Free Labor vs. Slavery in British Emancipation.* Oxford: Oxford University Press.

Drescher, Seymour, and Engerman, Stanley L. (eds.). 1998. *A Historical Guide to World Slavery.* New York: Oxford University Press.

Dubois, Laurent. 2004a. *A Colony of Citizens: Revolution and Slave Emancipation in the French Caribbean, 1787–1804.* Chapel Hill: University of North Carolina Press.

———. 2004b. *Avengers of the New World: The Story of the Haitian Revolution.* Cambridge, MA: Belknap Press.

Elkins, Stanley. 1959. *Slavery: A Problem in America Institutional and Intellectual Life.* Chicago: University of Chicago Press.

Eltis, David. 1983. "Free and Coerced Transatlantic Migrations: Some Comparisons." *American Historical Review* 88 (April), 251–80.

———. 1987. *Economic Growth and the Ending of the Transatlantic Slave Trade.* New York: Oxford University Press.

———. 2000. *The Rise of African Slavery in the Americas.* Cambridge: Cambridge University Press.

———. 2001. "The Volume and Structure of the Transatlantic Slave Trade: A Reassessment." *William and Mary Quarterly* 58 (January), 17–46.

Engerman, Stanley L. 1977. "Black Fertility and Family Structure in the United States, 1880–1940." *Journal of Family History* 2 (Summer), 117–38.

———. 1982. "Economic Adjustments to Emancipation in the United States and the British West Indies." *Journal of Interdisciplinary History* 13 (Autumn), 191–220.

———. 1984 . "Economic Change and Contract Labor in the British Caribbean: The End of Slavery and the Adjustment to Emancipation." *Explorations in Economic History* 21 (April), 133–50.

———. 1995. "Emancipations in Comparative Perspective: A Long and Wide View." In Gert Oostindie (ed.), *Fifty Years Later: Antislavery, Capitalism and Modernity in the Dutch Orbit.* Leiden: KITLV Press, 223–41.

———. 1996. "The Land and Labour Problem at the Time of the Legal Emancipation of British West Indian Slaves." In Roderick A. McDonald (ed.), *West Indies Accounts: Essays on the History of British Caribbean and the Atlantic Economy.* Kingston: The Press, University of the West Indies, 297–318.

———. 2000. "A Population History of the Caribbean." In Michael R. Haines and Richard H. Steckel (eds.), *A Population History of North America.* Cambridge: Cambridge University Press, 483–528.

———. 2002a. "Changing Laws and Regulations and Their Impact on Migration." In David Eltis (ed.), *Coerced and Free Migration: Global Perspectives.* Stanford: Stanford University Press, 75–93.

———. 2002b. "Labor Incentives and Manumission in Ancient Greek Slavery." In George Bitros and Yannis Katsoulacos (eds.), *Essays in Economic Theory, Growth, and Labor Markets.* Cheltenham: Edward Elgar, 211–19.

———. 2003. "The History and Political Economy of International Labor Standards." In Kaushik Basu et al. (eds.), *International Labor Standards: History, Theory and Policy Options.* Malden: Blackwell, 9–83.

———. 2007. "Voluntary Slavery." In K. Anthony Appiah and Martin Bunzl (eds.), *Buying Freedom: The Ethics and Economics of Slave Redemption.* Princeton: Princeton University Press.

———. Forthcoming. "Racism without Slavery, Slavery without Racism: Mainland North America and Elsewhere." In John Stauffer and Stanley L. Engerman (eds.), *Collective Degradation: Slavery and the Construction of Race.*

Engerman, Stanley L., and Higman, B. W. 1998. "The Demographic Structure of the Caribbean Slave Societies in the Eighteenth and Nineteenth Centuries." In Franklin W. Knight (ed.), *General His-*

tory of the Caribbean. Vol. 3. *The Slave Societies of the Caribbean.* London: UNESCO, 45–104.

Engerman, Stanley L., and Sokoloff, Kenneth L. 2002. "Factor Endowments, Inequality, and Paths of Development among New World Economies." *Economía* 3 (Fall), 41–88.

Engerman, Stanley L., and Sokoloff, Kenneth L. 2005. "The Evolution of Suffrage Institutions in the New World." *Journal of Economic History* 65 (December), 891–921.

Fass, Simon M. 1988. *Political Economy in Haiti: The Drama of Survival.* New Brunswick: Transaction Books.

Field, Daniel. 1976. *The End of Serfdom: Nobility and Bureaucracy in Russia, 1855–1861.* Cambridge, MA: Harvard University Press.

Fields, Barbara J. 1990. "Slavery, Race, and Ideology in the United States of America." *New Left Review* 181 (May/June), 95–118.

Finkelman, Paul, and Miller, Joseph C. (eds.). 1998. *Macmillan Encyclopedia of World Slavery.* New York: Macmillan Reference.

Finley, Moses I. 1976. "A Peculiar Institution?" *Times Literary Supplement,* July 2, 819–21. (Degler letter July 30, p. 958).

———. 1998. *Ancient Slavery and Modern Ideology* (expanded edition; first published 1980). Princeton: Markus Wiener.

Fitzgerald, Michael W. 2002. *Urban Emancipation: Popular Politics in Reconstruction Mobile, 1860–1890.* Baton Rouge: Louisiana State University Press.

Fladeland, Betty. 1976. "Compensated Emancipation: A Rejected Alternative." *Journal of Southern History* 42 (May), 169–86.

Fleming, Walter L. 1906–1907. *Documentary History of Reconstruction: Political, Military, Social, Religious, Educational and Industrial, 1865 to the Present Time.* Cleveland: Arthur H. Clark.

Fogel, Robert William. 1989. *Without Consent or Contract: The Rise and Fall of American Slavery.* New York: W. W. Norton.

———. 2003. *The Slavery Debates, 1952–1990: A Retrospective.* Baton Rouge: Louisiana State University Press.

Fogel, Robert William, and Engerman, Stanley L. 1974a. *Time on the Cross* (2 vols.). Boston: Little, Brown.

———. 1974b. "Philanthropy at Bargain Prices: Notes on the Economics of Gradual Emancipation." *Journal of Legal Studies* 3 (June), 377–401.

Foner, Eric. 1988. *Reconstruction: America's Unfinished Revolution, 1863–1877.* New York: Harper & Row.

Fox-Genovese, Elizabeth, and Genovese, Eugene D. 2005. *The Mind of the Master Class: History and Faith in the Southern Slaveholders' Worldview.* Cambridge: Cambridge University Press.

Franklin, John Hope, and Moss, Alfred A., Jr. 1994. *From Slavery to Freedom: A History of African Americans* (7th ed.). New York: Mc-Graw-Hill.

Frazier, E. Franklin. 1939. *The Negro Family in the United States.* Chicago: University of Chicago Press.

Fredrickson, George M. 1971. *The Black Image in the White Mind: The Debate on Afro-American Character and Destiny, 1817–1914.* New York: Harper & Row.

———. 2002. *Racism: A Short History.* Princeton: Princeton University Press.

Freedman, Paul. 1999. *Images of the Medieval Peasant.* Stanford: Stanford University Press.

Galenson, David W. 1981. *White Servitude in Colonial America: An Economic Analysis.* Cambridge: Cambridge University Press.

Gallay, Alan. 2002. *The Indian Slave Trade: The Rise of the English Empire in the American South, 1670–1717.* New Haven: Yale University Press.

Gardner, Ava. 1990. *Ava: My Story.* New York: Bantam Press.

Garnsey, Peter. 1996. *Ideas of Slavery from Aristotle to Augustine.* Cambridge: Cambridge University Press.

Genovese, Eugene D. 1974. *Roll, Jordan, Roll: The World the Slaves Made.* New York: Pantheon.

———. 1989. "The Southern Slaveholders' View of the Middle Ages." In Bernard Rosenthal and Paul E. Szarmach (eds.), *Medievalism in American Culture.* Binghamton: Center for Medieval and Renaissance Studies, SUNY–Binghamton, 31–52.

Green, William A. 1976. *British Slave Emancipation: The Sugar Colonies and the Great Experiment, 1830–1865.* Oxford: Clarendon Press.

Green-Pedersen, Svend E. 1975. "The History of the Danish Negro Slave Trade, 1733–1807: An Interim Survey Relating in Particular to Its Volume, Structure, Profitability and Abolition." *Revue d'histoire d'outre mer* 62 (no. 226–27), 196–220.

Grotius, Hugo. 1925. *The Law of War and Peace* (first published 1646). Oxford: Clarendon Press.

Gutman, Herbert G. 1976. *The Black Family in Slavery and Freedom, 1750–1925.* New York: Pantheon.

Hall, Douglas. 1959. *Free Jamaica, 1838–1865: An Economic History.* New Haven: Yale University Press.

Haring, C. H. 1947. *The Spanish Empire in America.* New York: Oxford University Press.

Hatcher, John. 1977. *Plague, Population, and the English Economy, 1348–1530.* London: Macmillan.

Hay, Douglas, and Craven, Paul (eds.). 2004. *Masters, Servants, and Magistrates in Britain and the Empire, 1562–1955.* Chapel Hill: University of North Carolina Press.

Heim, Carol E. 2000. "Structural Change: Regional and Urban." In Stanley L. Engerman and Robert E. Gallman (eds.), *The Cambridge Economic History of the United States,* vol. 3, *The Twentieth Century.* Cambridge: Cambridge University Press, 93–190.

Helg, Aline. 1995. *Our Rightful Share: The Afro-Cuban Struggle for Equality, 1886–1912.* Chapel Hill: University of North Carolina Press.

Hellie, Richard. 1982. *Slavery in Russia, 1450–1725.* Chicago: University of Chicago Press.

Helly, Denise (intro.). 1993. *The Cuba Commission Report: A Hidden History of the Chinese in Cuba* (first published 1876). Baltimore: Johns Hopkins University Press.

Higgs, Robert. 1977. *Competition and Coercion: Blacks in the American Economy, 1865–1914.* Cambridge: Cambridge University Press.

Hilton, R. H. 1969. *The Decline of Serfdom in Medieval England.* London: Macmillan.

Holloway, Thomas H. 1980. *Immigrants on the Land: Coffee and Society in São Paulo, 1886–1934.* Chapel Hill: University of North Carolina Press.

Holt, Sharon Ann. 2000. *Making Freedom Pay: North Carolina Freedpeople Working for Themselves, 1865–1900.* Athens: University of Georgia Press.

Holt, Thomas. 1977. *Black over White: Negro Political Leadership in South Carolina during Reconstruction.* Urbana: University of Illinois Press.

Hont, Istvan. 2005. *Jealousy of Trade: International Competition and the Nation-State in Historical Perspective.* Cambridge, MA: Belknap Press

Hudson, Larry E., Jr. 1997. *To Have and to Hold: Slave Work and Family Life in Antebellum South Carolina.* Athens: University of Georgia Press.

Huggins, Nathan I. 1977. *Black Odyssey: The Afro-American Ordeal in Slavery.* New York: Pantheon.

Hume, David. 1987. "Of Commerce" (first published 1752). In Eugene F. Miller (ed.), *Essays, Moral, Political, and Literary by David Hume.* Indianapolis: Liberty Fund, 253–67.

Hutcheson, Francis, 1968. *A System of Moral Philosophy.* (2 vols.; first published 1755; Hutcheson died in 1746). New York: A. M. Kelley.

Jordan, William Chester. 1986. *From Servitude to Freedom: Manumission in the Sénonais in the Thirteenth Century.* Philadelphia: University of Pennsylvania Press.

Karras, Ruth Mazo. 1988. *Slavery and Society in Medieval Scandinavia.* New Haven: Yale University Press.

Kennedy, Jos. C. G. 1862. *Preliminary Report on the Eighth Census, 1860.* Washington, D.C.: Government Printing Office.

Kenzer, Robert C. 1997. *Enterprising Southerners: Black Economic Success in North Carolina, 1865–1915.* Charlottesville: University Press of Virginia.

Keyssar, Alexander. 2000. *The Right to Vote: The Contested History of Democracy in the United States.* New York: Basic Books.

Kingston-Mann, Esther. 1999. *In Search of the True West: Culture, Economics, and Problems of Russian Development.* Princeton: Princeton University Press.

Klein, Herbert S. 1986. *African Slavery in Latin America and the Caribbean.* New York: Oxford University Press.

Klein, Martin A. 1990. "The Impact of the Atlantic Slave Trade on the Societies of the Western Sudan." *Social Science History* 14 (Summer), 231–53.

——— (ed.). 1993. *Breaking the Chains: Slavery, Bondage, and Emancipation in Modern Africa and Asia.* Madison: University of Wisconsin Press.

———. 1998. *Slavery and Colonial Rule in French West Africa.* Cambridge: Cambridge University Press.

———. 2002. *Historical Dictionary of Slavery and Abolition.* Lanham: Scarecrow Press.

Kolchin, Peter. 1987. *Unfree Labor: American Slavery and Russian Serfdom.* Cambridge, MA: Belknap Press.

Kousser, J. Morgan. 1974. *The Shaping of Southern Politics: Suffrage Restriction and the Establishment of the One-Party South, 1880–1910.* New Haven: Yale University Press.

Kuitenbrouwer, Maarten. 1995. "The Dutch Case of Antislavery: Late Abolitions and Elitist Abolitionism." In Gert Oostindie (ed.), *Fifty Years Later: Antislavery, Capitalism and Modernity in the Dutch Orbit.* Leiden: KITLV, 67–88.

Kulikoff, Allan. 1983. "Uprooted Peoples: Black Migrants in the Age of the American Revolution, 1790–1820." In Ira Berlin and Ronald Hoffman (eds.), *Slavery and Freedom in the Age of the American Revolution*. Charlottesville: University Press of Virginia, 143–71.

Lakwete, Angela. 2003. *Inventing the Cotton Gin: Machine and Myth in Antebellum America*. Baltimore: Johns Hopkins University Press.

Lauber, Almon Wheeler. 1913. *Indian Slavery in Colonial Times within the Present Limits of the United States*. New York: Columbia University Press.

Laurence, K. O. 1994. *A Question of Labour: Indentured Immigration into Trinidad and British Guiana, 1875–1917*. London: James Currey.

Lebergott, Stanley. 1964. *Manpower in Economic Growth: The American Record since 1800*. New York: McGraw-Hill.

Lecky, William Edward Hartpole. 1869. *A History of European Morals from Augustus to Charlemagne* (2 vols.). London: Longmans Green.

Lewis, Bernard. 1990. *Race and Slavery in the Middle East: An Historical Enquiry*. New York: Oxford University Press.

Leyburn, James G. 1941. *The Haitian People*. New Haven: Yale University Press.

Lincoln, Abraham. 1989a. *Speeches and Writings, 1832–1858*. New York: Library of America.

———. 1989b. *Speeches and Writings, 1859–1865*. New York: Library of America.

Lindert, Peter H. 2004. *Growing Public: Social Spending and Economic Growth since the Eighteenth Century* (2 vols.). Cambridge: Cambridge University Press.

Litwack, Leon F. 1961. *North of Slavery: The Negro in the Free States, 1790–1860*. Chicago: University of Chicago Press.

Locke, Mary S. 1901. *Anti-slavery in America from the Introduction of African Slaves to the Prohibition of the Slave Trade, 1619–1808*. Boston: Ginn.

Lockhart, James, and Schwartz, Stuart B. 1983. *Early Latin America: A History of Colonial Spanish America and Brazil.* Cambridge: Cambridge University Press.

Look Lai, Walton. 1993. *Indentured Labour, Caribbean Sugar: Chinese and Indian Migrants to the British West Indies, 1838–1918.* Baltimore: Johns Hopkins University Press.

Lovejoy, Paul E. 1983. *Transformations in Slavery: A History of Slavery in Africa.* Cambridge: Cambridge University Press.

Lovejoy, Paul E., and Hogendorn, Jan S. 1993. *Slow Death for Slavery: The Course of Abolition in Northern Nigeria, 1897–1936.* Cambridge: Cambridge University Press.

Lowenfish, Lee. 1991. *The Imperfect Diamond: A History of Baseball's Labor Wars* (rev. ed.). New York: Da Capo Press.

Maddison, Angus. 2001. *The World Economy: A Millennial Perspective.* Paris: OECD.

Manning, Patrick. 1988. *Francophone Sub-Saharan Africa, 1880–1985.* Cambridge: Cambridge University Press.

———. 1990. *Slavery and African Life: Occidental, Oriental and African Slave Trades.* Cambridge: Cambridge University Press.

Margo, Robert A. 1990. *Race and Schooling in the South, 1880–1950.* Chicago: University of Chicago Press.

Mattoso, Kátia M. de Queirós, Klein, Herbert S., and Engerman, Stanley L. 1986. "Trends and Patterns in the Prices of Manumitted Slaves, Bahia, 1819–1888." *Slavery and Abolition* 7 (May), 59–67.

Mazumdar, Sucheta. 1998. *Sugar and Society in China: Peasants, Technology, and the World Market.* Cambridge, MA: Harvard University Asia Center.

McGlynn, Frank (ed.). 1989. *Perspectives on Manumission* in *Slavery and Abolition* 10 (December), 1–128.

Miers, Suzanne. 2003. *Slavery in the Twentieth Century: The Evolution of a Global Pattern.* Walnut Creek: Rowman & Littlefield.

———. 2004. "Slave Rebellion and Resistance in the Aden Protectorate in the Mid-Twentieth Century." *Slavery and Abolition* 25 (August), 80–89.

Miers, Suzanne, and Roberts, Richard (eds.). 1988. *The End of Slavery in Africa.* Madison: University of Wisconsin Press.

Miller, Joseph C. (ed.). 1999. *Slavery and Slaving in World History: A Bibliography* (2 vols.). New York: M. E. Sharpe.

Moon, David. 2001. *The Abolition of Serfdom in Russia, 1762–1907.* New York: Longman.

Moreno Fraginals, Manuel. 1976. *The Sugar Mill: The Socioeconomic Complex of Sugar in Cuba, 1760–1860.* New York: Monthly Review Press.

———. 1986. "Plantation Economies and Societies in the Spanish Caribbean, 1860–1930." In Leslie Bethell (ed.), *The Cambridge History of Latin America,* vol. 4, c. 1870 to 1930. Cambridge: Cambridge University Press, 187–231.

Moreno Fraginals, Manuel, Klein, Herbert S., and Engerman, Stanley L. 1983. "The Level and Structure of Slave Prices on Cuban Plantations in the Middle of the Nineteenth Century: Some Comparative Perspectives." *American Historical Review* 88 (December), 1201–18.

Morgan, Philip D. 1982. "Work and Culture: The Task System and the World of Low Country Blacks, 1700 to 1880," *William and Mary Quarterly* 39 (October), 563–99.

Moya Pons, Frank. 1995. *The Dominican Republic: A National History.* New Rochelle: Hispaniola Books.

Murray, David R. 1980. *Odious Commerce: Britain, Spain, and the Abolition of the Cuban Slave Trade.* Cambridge: Cambridge University Press.

Nash, Gary B. 1990. *Race and Revolution.* Madison: Madison House.

Nelson, Lowry. 1950. *Rural Cuba.* Minneapolis: University of Minnesota Press.

Nevins, Allan. 1950. *The Emergence of Lincoln,* vol. 1: *Douglas, Buchanan, and Party Chaos, 1857–1859.* New York: Scribner.

Nicholls, David. 1979. *From Dessalines to Duvalier: Race, Colour and National Independence in Haiti.* Cambridge: Cambridge University Press.

Nieboer, H. J. 1971. *Slavery as an Industrial System; Ethnological Research* (2nd rev. ed.; first published 1910). New York: Burt Franklin.

Noggle, Burl. 1992. *The Fleming Lectures, 1937–1990: A Historiographical Essay.* Baton Rouge: Louisiana State University Press.

North, Douglass C. 1961. *The Economic Growth of the United States, 1790–1860.* Englewood Cliffs: Prentice-Hall.

Northrup, David. 1995. *Indentured Labor in the Age of Imperialism, 1834–1922.* Cambridge: Cambridge University Press.

Novak, William J. 1996. *The People's Welfare: Law and Regulation in Nineteenth-Century America.* Chapel Hill: University of North Carolina Press.

Oubre, Claude F. 1978. *Forty Acres and a Mule: The Freedmen's Bureau and Black Land Ownership.* Baton Rouge: Louisiana State University Press.

Outram, Dorinda. 2005. *The Enlightenment* (2nd ed.). Cambridge: Cambridge University Press.

Parliament of the Commonwealth of Australia. 1912. *Report of the Royal Commission on the Sugar Industry.* Government of the Commonwealth of Australia.

Patterson, Orlando. 1982. *Slavery and Social Death: A Comparative Study.* Cambridge, MA: Harvard University Press.

———. 1991. *Freedom in the Making of Western Culture.* New York: Basic Books.

Penningroth, Dylan C. 2003. *The Claims of Kinfolk: African American Property and Community in the Nineteenth-Century South.* Chapel Hill: University of North Carolina Press.

Philbrick, Francis S. (ed.). 1950. *The Laws of Illinois Territory, 1809–1818.* Springfield: Illinois State Historical Library.

Phillips, William D., Jr., and Phillips, Carla Rahn. 1992. *The Worlds of Christopher Columbus.* Cambridge: Cambridge University Press.

Porter, Dale H. 1970. *The Abolition of the Slave Trade in England, 1784–1807.* Hamden: Archon Books.

Price, Richard (ed.). 1973. *Maroon Societies: Rebel Slave Communities in the Americas.* Garden City: Anchor Press.

Pufendorf, Samuel. 1991. *On the Duty of Man and Citizen According to Natural Law* (first published 1673). Cambridge: Cambridge University Press.

Quirk, James, and Fort, Rodney D. 1992. *Pay Dirt: The Business of Professional Team Sports.* Princeton: Princeton University Press.

Rabinowitz, Howard N. 1978. *Race Relations in the Urban South, 1865–1890.* New York: Oxford University Press.

Ragsdale, Bruce A., and Treese, Joel D. 1990. *Black Americans in Congress, 1870–1989.* Washington, D.C.: Government Printing Office.

Roberts, G. W. 1955. "Emigration from the Island of Barbados." *Social and Economic Studies* 4 (September), 245–88.

———. 1957. *The Population of Jamaica.* Cambridge: Cambridge University Press.

Roberts, G. W., and Byrne, J. 1966. "Summary Statistics on Indenture and Associated Migration Affecting the West Indies, 1834–1918." *Population Studies* 20(July), 125–34.

Robinson, Randall. 2000. *The Debt: What America Owes to Blacks.* New York: Dutton.

Rodney, Walter. 1972. *How Europe Underdeveloped Africa.* London: Bogle-L'Ouverture Publications.

Rodrigue, John C. 2001. *Reconstruction in the Cane Fields: From Slavery to Free Labor in Louisiana's Sugar Parishes, 1862–1880.* Baton Rouge: Louisiana State University Press.

Rodriguez, Junius P. (ed.). 1997. *The Historical Encyclopedia of World Slavery* (2 vols.). Santa Barbara: ABC-CLIO.

———. 1999. *Chronology of World Slavery.* Santa Barbara: ABC-CLIO.

Roediger, David R. 1999. "Frederick Douglass Meets the Slavery Metaphor: Race, Labor, and Gender in the Languages of Antebellum Social Protest." In Stanley Engerman (ed.), *Terms of Labor: Slavery, Serfdom, and Free Labor.* Stanford: Stanford University Press, 168–87.

Rotberg, Robert I. 1971. *Haiti: The Politics of Squalor.* Boston: Houghton Mifflin.

Rousseau, Jean-Jacques. 1997. *The Social Contract and Other Later Political Writings.* Cambridge: Cambridge University Press.

Rout, Leslie B. 1976. *The African Experience in Spanish America: 1502 to the Present Day.* Cambridge: Cambridge University Press.

Rozbicki, Michael J. 2001. "To Save Them from Themselves: Proposals to Enslave the British Poor, 1698–1775." *Slavery and Abolition* 22 (August), 29–58.

Rusk, Jerrold G. 2001. *A Statistical History of the American Electorate.* Washington, D.C.: CQ Press.

Sacerdote, Bruce. 2005. "Slavery and the Intergenerational Transmission of Human Capital." *Review of Economics and Statistics* 87 (May), 217–34.

Schafer, Judith Kelleher. 2003. *Becoming Free, Remaining Free: Manumission and Enslavement in New Orleans, 1846–1862.* Baton Rouge: Louisiana State University Press.

Schroeder, Susan. 1982. *Cuba: A Handbook of Historical Statistics.* Boston: G. K. Hall.

Schweninger, Loren. 1990. *Black Property Owners in the South, 1790–1915.* Urbana: University of Illinois Press.

Scott, Rebecca J. 1985. *Slave Emancipations in Cuba: The Transition to Free Labor, 1860–1899.* Princeton: Princeton University Press.

———. 2005. *Degrees of Freedom: Louisiana and Cuba after Slavery.* Cambridge, MA: Belknap Press.

Sewell, William G. 1862. *The Ordeal of Free Labor in the British West Indies.* London: Sampson, Low.

Shepherd, James F., and Walton, Gary M. 1972. *Shipping, Maritime Trade, and the Economic Development of Colonial North America.* Cambridge: Cambridge University Press.

Sitterson, J. Carlyle. 1953. *Sugar Country: The Cane Sugar Industry in the South, 1753–1950.* Lexington: University of Kentucky Press.

Skinner, Quentin. 2002. "Classical Liberty and the Coming of the English Civil War." In Martin van Gelderen and Quentin Skinner (eds.), *Republicanism: A Shared European Heritage.* Vol. 2. *The Values of Republicanism in Early Modern Europe.* Cambridge: Cambridge University Press, 9–28.

Smith, Adam. 1976. *The Wealth of Nations* (2 vols.; first published 1776). Oxford: Clarendon Press.

———. 1978. *Lectures on Jurisprudence.* Oxford: Clarendon Press.

Stark, Rodney. 2003. *For the Glory of God: How Monotheism Led to Reformations, Science, Witch-Hunts, and the End of Slavery.* Princeton: Princeton University Press.

Starobin, Robert S. 1970. *Industrial Slavery in the Old South.* New York: Oxford University Press.

Steinfeld, Robert J. 1991. *The Invention of Free Labor: The Employment Relation in English and American Law and Culture, 1350–1870.* Chapel Hill: University of North Carolina Press.

———. 2001. *Coercion, Contract, and Free Labor in the Nineteenth Century.* Cambridge: Cambridge University Press.

Steuart, Sir James. 1966. *An Inquiry into the Principles of Political Economy* (2 vols.; first published 1767). Chicago: University of Chicago Press.

Stevenson, Brenda E. 1996. *Life in Black and White: Family and Community in the Slave South.* New York: Oxford University Press.

Sturge, Joseph, and Harvey, Thomas. 1968. *The West Indies in 1837* (first published in 1838). London: Cass.

Tannenbaum, Frank. 1946. *Slave and Citizen: The Negro in the Americas.* New York: Vintage Books.

Tawney, R. H. 1972. *Commonplace Book.* Cambridge: Cambridge University Press.

Temperley, Howard. 1972. *British Antislavery, 1833–1870.* London: Longman.

———. 1977. "Capitalism, Slavery and Ideology." *Past and Present* 75 (May), 94–118.

Thernstrom, Stephan, and Thernstrom, Abigail. 1997. *America in Black and White: One Nation, Indivisible.* New York: Simon & Schuster.

Tinker, Hugh. 1974. *A New System of Slavery: The Export of Indian Labour Overseas, 1830–1920.* London: Oxford University Press.

Tocqueville, Alexis de. 1840. *Report Made to the Chamber of Deputies on the Abolition of Slavery in the French Colonies, July 23, 1839.* Boston: J. Munroe.

———. 2001. *Writings on Empire and Slavery.* Edited by Jennifer Pitts. Baltimore: Johns Hopkins University Press. See "The Emancipation of Slaves" (first published 1843), 199–226.

Tolnay, Stewart E., and Beck, E. M. 1995. *A Festival of Violence: An Analysis of Southern Lynchings, 1882–1930.* Urbana: University of Illinois Press.

Tomlins, Christopher L. 1985. *The State and the Unions: Labor Relations, Law, and the Organized Labor Movement in America, 1880–1960.* Cambridge: Cambridge University Press.

Trefousse, Hans L. 1997. *Thaddeus Stevens: Nineteenth-Century Egalitarian.* Chapel Hill: University of North Carolina Press.

Tucker, George. 1855. *Progress of the United States in Population and Wealth in Fifty Years.* New York: Press of Hunt's Merchants' Magazine.

van den Anker, Christen (ed.). 2004. *The Political Economy of New Slavery.* Houndmills: Palgrave Macmillan.

Van Deusen, Glydon G. 1953. *Horace Greeley: Nineteenth-Century Crusader.* Philadelphia: University of Philadelphia Press.

Vaughan, Alden T. 1995. *Roots of American Racism: Essays on the Colonial Experience.* New York: Oxford University Press.

Vincent, Charles. 1976. *Black Legislators in Louisiana during Reconstruction.* Baton Rouge: Louisiana State University Press.

Voegeli, V. Jacque. 2003. "A Rejected Alternative: Union Policy and the Relocation of Southern 'Contrabands' at the Dawn of Emancipation." *Journal of Southern History* 69 (November), 765–90.

Walker, Francis A. 1872. *A Compendium of the Ninth Census (June 1, 1870).* Washington, D.C.: Government Printing Office.

Wang, Xi. 1997. *The Trial of Democracy: Black Suffrage and Northern Republicans, 1860–1910.* Athens: University of Georgia Press.

Watson, James (ed.). 1980. *Asian and African Systems of Slavery.* Oxford: Basil Blackwell.

Weber, Max. 1976. *The Agrarian Sociology of Ancient Civilizations* (first published 1896). Atlantic Highlands: Humanities Press.

Whatley, Christopher A. 2000. *Scottish Society, 1707–1830: Beyond Jacobitism, towards Industrialisation.* Manchester: Manchester University Press.

Wiedemann, Thomas. 1981. *Greek and Roman Slavery.* Baltimore: Johns Hopkins University Press.

Wilberforce, William. 1807. *A Letter on the Abolition of the Slave Trade.* London: Luke Hansard.

Williams, David (ed.). 1999. *The Enlightenment.* Cambridge: Cambridge University Press.

Williams, Eric. 1944. *Capitalism and Slavery.* Chapel Hill: University of North Carolina Press.

———. 1966. *British Historians and the West Indies.* London: Andre Deutsch.

Williamson, Joel. 1984. *The Crucible of Race: Black-White Relations in the American South since Emancipation.* Oxford: Oxford University Press.

Wilson, James Q. 2002. "Slavery and the Black Family." *The Public Interest* 147 (Spring), 3–23.

Wilson, Theodore. 1965. *The Black Codes of the South.* University: University of Alabama Press.

Wilson, William Julius. 1987. *The Truly Disadvantaged: The Inner City, the Underclass, and Public Policy.* Chicago: University of Chicago Press.

Wolf, John B. 1979. *The Barbary Coast: Algiers under the Turks, 1500–1830.* New York: W. W. Norton.

Woodman, Harold D. 1995. *New South, New Law: The Legal Foundations of Credit and Labor Relations in the Postbellum Agricultural South.* Baton Rouge: Louisiana State University Press.

Woodward, C. Vann. 1974. *The Strange Career of Jim Crow* (3rd rev. ed.). New York: Oxford University Press.

Wright, Gavin. 1978. *The Political Economy of the Cotton South: Households, Markets, and Wealth in the Nineteenth Century.* New York: W. W. Norton.

Wright, Quincy. 1965. *A Study of War* (2nd ed.). Chicago: University of Chicago Press.

Xenophon. 1990. *Conversation of Socrates.* Harmondsworth: Penguin Books.

Young, Arthur. 1772. *Political Essays Concerning the Present State of the British Empire.* London: W. Strahan & T. Cadell

Zilversmit, Arthur. 1967. *The First Emancipation: The Abolition of Slavery in the North.* Chicago: University of Chicago Press.

Ziskind, David. 1993. *Emancipation Acts: Quintessential Labor Laws.* Los Angeles: Litlaw Foundation.